GHOST STORIES
of Washington

BARBARA SMITH

LONE
PINE

The Publisher: Lone Pine Publishing

10145 - 81 Avenue	1901 Raymond Ave. SW, Suite C
Edmonton, AB T6E 1W9	Renton, WA 98055
Canada	USA

Website: www.lonepinepublishing.com

Canadian Cataloguing in Publication Data
Smith, Barbara, 1947 –
     Ghost stories of Washington

Includes bibliographical references.
     ISBN 1-55105-260-1

     1. Ghosts—Washington (State). 2. Legends—Washington (State). I. Title.
GR580.S668 2000   398.2'0979705   C99-911238-4

Editorial Director: Nancy Foulds
Project Editor: Randy Williams
Production Manager: Jody Reekie
Book Design, Layout & Production: Monica Triska
Photos Courtesy of: Lone Pine Publishing (p. 15); Manresa Castle (p. 75); E.R. Rogers Mansion (p. 70, 85); Steilacoom Historical Association (p. 94, 95); Robert Smith (p. 106, 205); Dana Cox, Historian for the Seattle Underground (pp. 110); Dr. Wayne McVey (pp. 103, 122, 149, 188, 199, 202); Mount Baker Theatre (pp. 129, 139, 140, 141, 175); The Capitol Theatre (pp. 145).

We acknowledge the financial support of the Government of Canada through the Book Publishing Industry Development Program (BPIDP) for our publishing activities.

PC: P6

Dedication

This book is dedicated to my friend Michael Jorgensen, a native of Washington and an extraordinarily talented filmmaker.

For my grandsons and their peers—who will need forests as much as books—arrangements have been made to plant trees to compensate for the paper used in printing this volume.

Contents

Chapter 3: Ghosts in Public

Chapter 4: Stage Fright

Chapter 5: The Road Well Traveled

Acknowledgments

It would not be possible for me to write any of my books without the cooperation of many other people. For this reason, some books are easier to complete than others. This book was a delight to work on from beginning to end. Time and time again, the people of Washington went well out of their way to supply me with the documents and information I needed.

To all the folks mentioned in the stories, many thanks for your friendly support. It is much appreciated. Some people, for understandable reasons, asked to remain anonymous. You, of course, will not be named—but you are thanked, warmly. Thanks are also extended to the talented paranormal investigators who have gone before. These people, who are often local experts, have done an invaluable job of researching possible explanations for particular hauntings. As a storyteller and folklore collector, my experience has been significantly enriched by their groundbreaking efforts.

In addition, I was assisted through the generosity and kindness of the following individuals: Paranormal researcher extraordinaire, W. Ritchie Benedict of Calgary, Alberta, whose talents and generosity are amazing. Fellow author (and dear friend) Jo-Anne Christensen of Edmonton, Alberta, who shared both resources and ideas with me. Dana Cox, of the Seattle Underground, has been a joy to work with throughout several of my projects; this time she even supplied me with further story leads. Joan Curtis, of the Steilacoom Historical Society, dug around until she found the photographs I was after. Dr. Wayne McVey of Edmonton went out of his way to take several photographs that I needed. Thank you, Wayne, and my apologies to both you and your wife, Diane, for having interfered with your trip! Dr. Barrie Robinson of

Edmonton generously offered research and editorial guidance. Mary Lou Skinner Ross, of Issaquah, Washington, went to the trouble of following up a request that was really no more than a shot in the dark. My husband, Bob Smith, attended to many supportive (and often thankless!) chores for me. My tasks would have been much more difficult to accomplish without help from the staff of Edmonton Public Library, particularly at Idylwylde Branch and the Interlibrary Loan Department.

My efforts, and those of the people named above, would have been in vain without the amazing support that I receive from the talented people who make up the staff at Lone Pine Publishing. When a group of authors get together, the first item of discussion is typically to complain about some aspect of the publishing firm with whom they're working. Throughout such discussions I must remain mute, for I have the pleasure of being supported by, in my opinion, the best possible publisher. Warm thanks to all at Lone Pine. Your efforts on my behalf are always deeply appreciated. Special mention must go to Helen Ibach and Rick Truppner of the Washington office—thank you for so promptly and thoroughly responding to my queries.

Introduction

I was intrigued by some of the ghosts in Washington long before I began writing books of ghost stories. Years ago, while enjoying a tour of the Seattle Underground, I came away convinced that place was haunted. To examine my conviction a bit further, I wrote a couple of magazine articles about the area. Those assignments left me wanting to investigate the ghostlore in Washington even further. I was therefore delighted to be given the opportunity to work on this book.

Compiling and writing *Ghost Stories of Washington* proved to be even more fun than I had hoped it would be. Quite often I would follow up one lead only to discover yet another intriguing ghost story. The tales that made the final cut for this book are, I hope, representative of both the history and geography of the state. In addition, I've tried to choose stories that exemplify several different types of ghosts and hauntings.

While the wide variety of haunting tales I found in Washington was certainly gratifying, it also means that the author and the readers should agree to share a definition of the word "ghost." Although I've devoted considerable effort over the past 10 years to formalizing just such a definition, I'm no closer to my goal now than when I started. Unfortunately, this lack of certainty extends to several related—and possibly unanswerable—questions. Why are ghosts here? Why are some people so much more likely than others to see a ghost? Why are some locations haunted while others places where equally traumatic events have occurred remain "cold," uninhabited by spirits?

Although my investigations have not supplied me with the concise definition I was after, they have taught me what a ghost is not. A ghost is not a cute, white cartoon character, nor is it a human figure draped in a sheet. A ghost is also not necessarily a filmy, gauzy apparition—although some certainly do fit that description. Ghosts do not exist to scare us. I firmly believe that most of these otherworldly presences are simply unaware—or unwilling to accept—that they are no longer living. Other ghosts, however, seem to haunt for a particular purpose. I found so many of this last kind of spirit in Washington that an entire section of this book is made up of "Phantoms With a Mission" (pp. 205-230).

Other stories, such as "The Ghosts Underground" (p. 105), are excellent examples of energy having been recorded, or embedded, on the environment in which an event has occurred. This recording is simply replayed over and over again on the psychic landscape. Not all people are aware of this phenomenon at all times, but, like the sound waves made by the tree falling in an empty forest, such a place has experienced vibrations nonetheless. It has become haunted.

Admittedly, differentiating between a place that is truly haunted and one that experiences one or more visitations from a ghost leads us into the treacherous waters of semantics. I hope that the differences between some of the incidents described in this book will be dramatic enough to clarify my point. One further opportunity for confusion remains. Although there are few true synonyms in the English language, I have chosen to use the following words interchangeably: specter, spirit, entity, presence, manifestation, phantom, wraith, vision, image, shade, revenant and ghost.

Not all ghosts present themselves visually. Those that do are more properly called "apparitions." Just because a ghost is not seen, however, does not mean there isn't one present. A spirit may manifest itself as nothing more than a sensation—that creeping feeling that one is not alone even though no one else is physically present. An unexplainable odor—either pleasant or unpleasant—may also indicate that a ghost is nearby. Other evidence of paranormal occurrences can include ghostly lights and phantom music.

A "poltergeist" is a rare type of spectral being that can be identified by its noisy and even violent behavior. This type of ghost will often move objects with great force and can wreak considerable havoc on its surrounding environment. Poltergeists are associated with individuals rather than with places. They have been known to follow people for years, even through a succession of moves from one residence to another.

"Retrocognition" (also known as postcognition), which is described as seeing or sensing the past, is a particularly fascinating type of ghostly encounter. Some students of the paranormal believe that most, if not all, hauntings are a result of retrocognition. The phenomenon is thought to be the result of a temporary displacement in time that gives the person affected an opportunity to review or experience historical events. Retrocognition probably occurs much more frequently than is commonly recognized because fleeting temporal displacement is often written off as a figment of the witness's imagination. Perhaps we should pay closer attention to momentary shifts in our perception when we experience them.

The opposite of retrocognition is "precognition"—seeing or sensing an event that has not yet occurred. When such an experience is accompanied by a presence, that presence is called a "forerunner."

One final type of phantom energy is the manifestation of ghost lights, or ignes fatui. These luminous paranormal occurrences have entranced people over the centuries.

But why do these, or any, ghostly phenomena exist? The theory of "leftover energy"—both physical and emotional—is frequently used to explain the existence of ghosts. This theory is related to the concept of "psychic imprint"—the idea that the essence of a person or an event has somehow been "stamped" onto the environment in which that person lived or the event occurred.

The deceased person's soul has effectively left an imprint on the physical world. He or she has become a ghost. Traumatic or violent events can also leave such a mark, resulting in a specific place being haunted.

Another theory holds that ghosts are disembodied souls (or energies, personalities or spirits) that are usually detectable only by our nearly atrophied "sixth sense." Rather than perceiving this otherworldly sensation with our usual and familiar five senses, we may only notice the hair on our arms or on the back of our necks standing on end, or be aware of a tingling sensation in our skin. Alternatively, we might experience the decidedly disconcerting feeling that we are not alone or that we are being watched, even though our other senses fail to confirm the existence of another presence near us.

Scientists have suggested that humans really do possess a rarely used sixth sense, located in the vomeronasal organ of the nose. This organ is capable of detecting pheromones, which are chemicals released into the air in small quantities by many species as a way of communicating with others of their kind.

Perhaps the vomeronasal organ also detects energy exuded by disembodied spirits but, because we are not accustomed to consciously receiving signals from the sixth sense, we do not recognize the messages as anything more than a vague awareness that "something" is close by. Youngsters seem to be more sensitive to otherworldly presences than are adults. Perhaps this is because children are more sensitive to stimuli received from their vomeronasal organs. Over time, adults come to rely almost exclusively on their other five senses and therefore typically ignore—or fail to respond to—sensations picked up by their sixth sense. Those adults who do recognize and rely upon such messages are often referred to as "sensitives." Though this sensitivity seems to be inborn, it can apparently be enhanced with practice—or diminished through neglect. Perhaps the variations in sensitivity from person to person explain why some people are much more likely than others to encounter a ghost.

Beyond all of these suppositions lurks a further mystery: Does a ghostly event originate with the living person who is experiencing the encounter, or with the ghost itself? Perhaps that point is debatable but, because many people have reported seeing (or sensing) the same spirits at different times, the entities and events chronicled in this book are unlikely to be mere figments of the observers' imaginations.

Being haunted is not necessarily a permanent status for either a person or a place. A location that is currently haunted may not always be so. Conversely, just because your home and workplace are now ghost-free zones, there is no guarantee that they will remain in that condition indefinitely.

Some ghosts and hauntings are incredibly tenacious. For example, the ghosts of Roman soldiers are still occasionally spotted roaming the English countryside where they battled centuries ago, but few ghosts are that ancient. Because I have never heard of or read about any place or person being haunted by the ghost of a prehistoric cave dweller, I presume that, like all forms of energy, ghosts eventually weaken and dissipate.

In the presence of a ghost or during an active haunting, observers will usually note predictable and distinguishable changes in the environment. Such changes often include a sudden, dramatic temperature drop that is very localized, though it may encompass a large area. Drafts, odors or noises—all of which are apparently sourceless—may also be present.

Despite the lack of agreement on what a ghost might be, ghosts exist in all cultures and have been noted throughout history. My personal experience collecting ghost stories has taught me one other consistency: A paranormal encounter is a profoundly moving event. I have yet to have a story told to me in a flippant or matter-of-fact manner. Out of respect for this emotional factor, I have agreed to protect a contributor's anonymity whenever he or she has requested that I do so.

The narratives in this book are reports of real events. We all know that life, as we live it, is anything but neat and tidy. As a result, these accounts tend to be a bit more ragged than the stories we are used to reading. A fictional tale of a haunting will be structured with a predictable presentation: a beginning, a middle and an end. The anecdotes recorded here refuse to be that orderly. Oftentimes they are merely fragments, which can be somewhat frustrating in a world so fond of tidy resolutions. We tend to find narratives more satisfying when loose ends are neatly tied up in the last sentence of a tale. However, in those cases where there is not enough information to tell a traditional story, the parts that are missing can be every bit as provocative as the parts that are known.

This collection is not intended as an attempt to replace anyone's personal belief system with my convictions or explanations. My intent is to entertain and to possibly prompt thought in areas that you might not have considered exploring otherwise. Though I do not pretend to be an educator, if reading this book introduces you to facets of Washington's history or geography with which you were previously unfamiliar, then I am delighted.

For the most part, I have excluded the Native American peoples' tales about spirits and the supernatural. Although these stories would definitely make a fascinating book, I am not qualified to write it.

If you have any additions to the stories contained here, or personal experiences with the paranormal that you would like to share with me, please contact me through Lone Pine Publishing. I'd love to hear from you. In the meantime, do enjoy this unique look at some of Washington's most unusual folklore.

Chapter 1

HAUNTED HOUSES

For most of us, our home is the single most important place in the world. No matter whether we live in a mansion or a hovel, it's "home," our ultimate shelter from the rigors of the world. Nowhere else do we find such security and comfort. Moreover, we often share our homes with those we love most. Perhaps, then, we shouldn't be too surprised that such an intimate, emotionally charged area is frequently the site of paranormal activity.

The emotional energy we exude becomes embedded in the psychic landscape surrounding us. If, in his lifetime, your father sat in a particular chair reading his newspaper every evening, you might, after his death, still think that you see him there occasionally. Such a sighting really begs a question: Does the image reside solely in the magination of the one perceiving it, or is a remnant of the dead man's spirit still enjoying the sports pages?

The following stories suggest that not all of the ethereal images in our homes are merely wishful memories. Some people truly do share their homes with ghosts.

World-famous Washington Story

Washington State has been home to some landmark hauntings. One of the strangest has to be the case of the haunted home of the Smith family (no relation to me).

Although this ghost story did not become public knowledge until the mid-1970s, terrifying events had already been taking place in the Seattle home for more than 10 years by that time. When Doris Smith bought the bungalow in 1962 as a home for herself and her two teenage children, the former owners gave her no indication that there was anything out of the ordinary about the little house.

The first hint that paranormal forces were at work came during the week between Christmas and New Year's Eve in 1962. Doris heard "noises and scraping of furniture." The woman's first thought was that an intruder had somehow broken into the house. Somewhat hesitantly, she checked all the rooms and found no one else present. Doris knew what she'd heard and knew that she was not the type who was given to flights of fantasy—but she would never have guessed at the time that she had purchased an extremely haunted piece of real estate and was about to go up against the challenge of her life. From then on, according to psychic investigator Bart Ellis, the "noises ... began to occur more regularly." Worse, the phantom sounds were often accompanied by unpleasant odors and malfunctions in electrical equipment.

Understandably concerned about her family's safety, Doris Smith began to ask her neighbors if they'd noticed anything strange in the area. Everyone she questioned reported that there was nothing at all unusual about their area—with the exception of the house that Doris had just purchased. The frightening events in that house, they told her, were the reason that the previous family had decided to move.

As Mrs. Smith struggled to comprehend her situation, the telltale signs of the haunting increased—and it was not just members of the Smith family who bore witness to the phantom activity. Anyone who happened to be in the house heard inexplicable screams, footsteps, disembodied voices—some of which were singing, others that were talking—and other, unidentified "strange noises." No matter where in the house a person happened to be, the sounds seemed to be coming from another location. If people were in the basement, they would hear ghostly voices from the living room. If the people went up to the living room, those same sounds would now seem to be coming from the basement.

The sounds of the haunting continued to be elusive—but before long the sights were not. Doris Smith, her children, and anyone else who happened to be in the house would stare in amazement as the doors to kitchen cupboards opened and closed, apparently of their own accord. Water gushed from faucets when no one had even been near the tap.

The family bravely tried to carry on with life as best they could, but when Doris began to see apparitions she became extremely concerned. She described shadows appearing on walls at a time and place when no shadow should have been possible. She and her family stood in amazement as "a smoke-shaped form" materialized in the entrance to one room. On different occasions, glowing red lights and a "shaft of light" manifested in the basement. Offensive odors would suddenly hang in the air and then, just as quickly, all traces would be gone.

In a hopeful attempt to find a "natural" cause and remedy for the strange goings-on, Doris Smith called in representatives of every conceivable trade. Much to her disappointment, none of the carpenters, plumbers or electricians she contracted could offer any physical explanation for the things that she was hearing, seeing and smelling.

In desperation, Doris Smith finally called in psychics. These people did have some answers for her, although it's doubtful that theirs were the answers she wanted. Margaret, the first psychic to tour the house, was immediately drawn to the living room—but as soon as she got there, she stopped dead in her tracks. Clutching her chest, the sensitive declared, "There is so much sadness in the house that it hurts my chest." At least the Smiths now knew they had not been imagining all of the bizarre things that had been happening in their home.

Margaret then put herself into a trance state and entered the basement bedroom used by Doris's son. Just seconds after she lay down on the teenager's bed, Margaret began to speak. Margaret told Doris, "The ghost who lives here is an Indian named Douglas. He lives at the house with his mother, whose name is Dove. Douglas is at the house to protect the bones of his ancestors, which are on the grounds. The ancestors were apparently killed by Oregon fur traders."

This information probably did not do much to comfort any of the Smiths, because it implied that the haunting was a long-term situation and that the ghosts were enduring. Margaret's next inferences, though, must have relieved Doris Smith's mind. Speaking in the peculiar fashion of someone in a trance-state, the psychic added that Douglas was also protecting another woman in the house, one who was "part Indian." Margaret had no prior knowledge of anyone living in the house, so she could not have known that Doris's heritage included Native American people. Doris took Margaret's words to mean that the spirit was also watching over her well-being.

Margaret spoke to Douglas directly, trying to assure him that the Smiths were looking after the house and the land on which it stood. She encouraged Douglas to leave his post as guard and go on to his final reward.

Still in an altered state of consciousness, Margaret and those accompanying her left the house and began to walk around the yard. After just a few moments, the psychic stopped and announced that human remains—most likely those from the massacre that Douglas's spirit had described—were buried just below her feet. She declared "the vibrations to be very strong" in two particular places. It was below those spots, she concluded, that the skeletons lay.

Less than a month after Margaret's visit, Doris Smith arranged to have another psychic, a man named Paul, come to the house. She took care to ensure that the man knew nothing about her or the house. She did not tell him of Margaret's recent findings or even of the other psychic's visit to the haunted house. Despite this secrecy, Paul went directly to the two places in the yard that Margaret had identified as being full of energy. He felt equally strong vibrations in those areas.

Being a pragmatic sort, Doris began to investigate the local history so she could verify the things that the psychics had told her. According to sources at the Seattle Public Library, there had been a terrible battle on the approximate site where her house stood. During the 1850s, Native American people camped in the area. History not only records battles between two tribes, but also between the Natives and the fur traders. Clearly, many lives had been lost on the land that Doris Smith now owned. Small wonder that her house was home to spirits as well as to the living.

By this time, word about the eerie events in the Seattle house had spread. Bart Ellis, a psychic investigator from Los Angeles, made arrangements to visit the Smiths and their noisy, uninvited phantom house guests. Armed with an ordinary portable tape recorder, Ellis visited the house many times between August 8 and 22, 1970. He came away with recordings that, to this day, shock anyone who listens to them, including me!

Ellis set the machine to the "record" setting, ensured that no one stayed behind in the basement, and then left. A constant roar of static and the sounds of people laughing, screaming and speaking are clearly audible, as are the sounds of footfalls and doors opening and closing. Interestingly, while Ellis was in the basement setting up his equipment he could not hear any noises at all.

On his last night at the haunted house, Ellis, with the support of Doris Smith, invited a party of interested people, including a scientist, a journalist, and a graduate student from the University of Washington, to join him in recording the ghostly sounds. A total of 14 tape recorders were set up and left to run while all involved sat upstairs together, never leaving the living room. All 14 recorders captured the same inexplicable sounds.

Later in the evening, the group, which also included a friend of Doris's, gathered in the basement room where their tape machines had been set up. Once assembled, they all heard the unmistakable sounds of someone walking on the floor above them—even though all of the living beings in the house were together on the lower level.

The graduate student offered to pace out the route the footsteps had taken while the others listened. He walked across the living room to the kitchen and then down the basement stairs. Those gathered then broke into two smaller groups, one staying downstairs and one up. The people upstairs could, of course, hear (as well as see) the student walking—but his single set of footfalls was all that they heard. The group in the basement heard two distinct sets of footsteps—the student's and the ghost's.

At this point in their exhausting day, Doris and her visiting friend were understandably tired. The researchers left and the two women sat quietly in a basement room, trying to absorb all that they had experienced over the last few hours. As they did, a "milky-white, cloudy, opaque light shaft" suddenly appeared.

Seeming to originate near the ceiling, it shone down and then moved along the floor, changing from a shaft to a circle of light. The circle appeared to be made up of many smaller circles of equally bright light. Terrified, Doris Smith's friend grabbed for a flashlight and aimed it at the presence—which then vanished before their eyes.

Once back in California, Bart Ellis took his tapes to be checked out by the Sony Corporation. Although the technicians could also hear the human voices, they were at a loss to explain them. Next he played the sounds for an anthropological linguist, who declared that the voices were not speaking in either a Germanic or Romance language, but in what was probably a North American aboriginal language.

Although the Smiths tried to adapt, it was difficult to function normally in a haunted house inhabited by spirits that were apparently gaining strength. Manifestations of pulsating, transparent white human-sized forms began appearing in different rooms of the house. A family friend captured the image of one of those supernatural presences with her camera. Once developed, the photograph clearly revealed a misty formation.

Even recreational activities were difficult in the house. When Mrs. Smith's son and his friends would try to play a game of pool in the basement gameroom, the cue ball would often move suddenly and mysteriously. Eventually the family gave up trying to play pool. But the boy's bedroom, which adjoined the gameroom, was sometimes filled with the distinct sounds of pool balls being hit by cues in the middle of the night. Whatever was in the house clearly did not want the living to play pool, yet it wanted to enjoy a game for itself.

Because nothing has been heard about this haunted house for many years now, it is reasonable to assume that the dead and the living eventually found mutually satisfying accommodations.

The Cat's in the Cottage

I began the research for this book by scattering requests for contributions all over the state. The following story took a convoluted route to reach me, and I'm extremely glad it arrived because this is a truly fascinating tale about a modern-day haunting.

Just a few years ago, a young couple we'll call Tim and Louise moved into what Louise described as "a studio cottage apartment in Seattle's south side." She went on to explain that the rental property was located in "a nice little complex of cottages, on the ground level with flowers and grass." She looked forward to enhancing the appearance of their new home by planting a flower garden in the front yard.

The pair settled in happily and was delighted when they discovered that they had been "adopted" by a stray cat in the neighborhood. "It loved to come inside the apartment," Louise remembered. "The cat had its favorite spots to lay in, as if it had been there before."

Neither Tim nor Louise objected to having a part-time pet. As a matter of fact, they quite enjoyed having the animal in their lives. About the same time they were being adopted by the critter, however, they both began to hear faint but disturbing noises. "It sounded like a woman moaning," Louise said.

At first the couple weren't terribly concerned by the slightly eerie sound. "We thought maybe it was just the neighbors," Louise recalled. Unfortunately for their peace of mind, the neighbors soon moved away. Worse, the moans did not merely continue— they actually became more intense.

According to Louise, the experience "was kind of creepy, but the idea that the apartment might be haunted was, at the same time, exciting. We didn't tell anyone about the moaning because we wanted to be sure that it wasn't just the pipes or some other mundane cause. We wanted to be sure that it was something more. It wasn't long before we got our proof."

Initially, that proof was subtle. On several occasions, both Tim and Louise were sure that pieces of their furniture had moved slightly, even though neither of them had touched anything. Soon, the entity became bolder. "There were a few times when I actually *saw* chairs move," Louise recalled.

Despite this visual evidence, the practical couple wanted more proof that what they believed they were seeing and sensing was not a product of their own imaginations. They set about constructing a homespun experiment.

"We would draw crayon circles around the legs of the chairs in the kitchen to make sure that we weren't just seeing things," Louise said. "A few minutes later, we'd check the chairs and find that they had moved right out of the circle."

Now they were certain that there was a manifestation of some sort in their home.

"One day [Tim] was home by himself with the cat. It had gotten into a fight with another cat and had its foot badly injured. [Tim] was on the couch holding the cat, trying to get a look at the animal's injured foot. The cat obviously didn't feel like being held at that moment and was trying to wriggle his foot away, meowing loudly in the process," Louise explained. "Then the moaning started."

"From the back of the apartment, a woman's voice started wailing 'nooooo' very loudly," she recalled. "Whatever was back there had picked up a large beach towel from the bathroom and thrown it into the kitchen, and had knocked other items around in the bathroom. Needless to say, [Tim] let the cat go."

As soon as he did, the eerie moaning stopped.

Tim and Louise deduced that their feline visitor belonged to whomever had lived in the suite before they moved in.

"We had been getting mail for someone named Alice for quite some time, so we figured she was our ghost. A couple of months later, I was talking to a neighbor and asked her about who had lived in our place before we did. She said that it was an old lady who had eight cats."

The neighbor added some provocative details. "One day the old lady was gone and management simply turned her cats loose," the neighbor said. No one knew for sure whether the old lady had died, only that she was gone abruptly.

The cat that Tim and Louise had befriended was apparently the old woman's favorite and the only one that stuck around after she was gone.

The couple's kindness to the animal, and their calm acceptance of a rather spooky situation seemed to increase the strength of the moaning spirit. In addition to hearing the old woman, Louise could now occasionally see what she presumed was the deceased woman's image. She described the sight as "something akin to a floating, dancing white rope."

The haunting continued for a few months before weakening. "The moaning was getting fainter," Louise recalled. "By the time we moved to a bigger apartment in the same complex, all the activity had stopped."

The little cottage-style apartment was no longer haunted.

The Presence

The early months of 1990 were exciting times for Jeff and Catherine Rollosson Halbhuber. In January of that year, they moved into their first home; in March, Alex, their first son, was born.

Catherine described the starter home as "a modest ranch-style house, about 15 years old" and added a particularly appealing description of its Seattle/Tacoma-area location. "I referred to it as a sub-rural neighborhood. It was developing, but there was still some farming around."

"Not long after our son was born, I began to notice that I was uncomfortable with the idea of spending time alone in the living room," Catherine remembered. When she mentioned these unusual feelings to Jeff, he admitted that he had been feeling much the same way. And, like his wife, Jeff Rollosson Halbhuber only felt uneasy in one room of the house—the living room.

"What was more disturbing was our son's reaction. He was the kind of baby who liked to be walked late at night. As he got older, he learned how to steer me where he wanted to go by pushing at me or leaning in the preferred direction," Catherine recalled. "Night after night, [Alex] would get me up and steer me down the hall to check out the living room. I would stop in every other room along the way, turning on lights and hoping he would be content with checking those."

Despite her best efforts, the infant "would insist on checking the living room." Catherine soon discovered that the baby didn't actually want to be in the living room. "Once we'd peeked in there, he would be content to return to his own room for rocking, nursing and pacing."

By now both Catherine and Jeff were fully aware that they were sharing their new home with more than just one another and an infant son. They began to call the unseen and unheard entity by the only name that felt reasonable—the Presence.

"This went on for a few months, although it never got worse than our feeling uncomfortable and unwelcome in the living room," Catherine said.

The sensation of being unwelcome in their own home—resented by something or someone they could only sense—must have been unpleasant, and Jeff and Catherine tried at first to expel the Presence.

"We tried a couple of different solutions," Catherine remembered. The couple had not discussed their unusual housing situation with very many of their friends, but one of the few who did know about it gave Jeff and Catherine a quartz ball. "It was a sphere," Catherine said. "It was small, maybe an inch in diameter, and was supposed to absorb the negative energy from the room."

When the couple continued to sense the Presence and feel unwelcome in the living room, Catherine tried another method of cleansing the area. "I tried making a 'witch bottle' with the same purpose in mind. This was actually something that I had read about in a book. It was just a small bottle that I put scraps of thread in. There was a little chant that you said with it which was meant, again, to absorb negative energy."

Catherine's attempts to rid her house of the unwanted guest failed, but the people and the Presence did eventually come to something like a truce. "It was just sort of a gradual acceptance. It got to the point where I was quite comfortable sewing in the living room by myself up to 2:00 AM," Catherine recalled. "Even so, I was quick to leave the room after turning the light off."

After six years, and for reasons not connected to the entity, the family made the difficult decision to move on. That, Catherine explained, was when things took a turn for the worse. "We had gotten an offer from another family with small children, and the Presence seemed content with that," she said. "But the offer went bad and we ended up selling the house to a young, unmarried man. We definitely got the feeling that the Presence was not very happy about this. We think [the entity] had come to like the presence of children in the house. There was a return of the dark feelings from our earliest days in the house. Nothing physical—there never was—just a sense that everything was not right."

Although few of their friends were aware of the being that Jeff or Catherine called the Presence, they discovered that they were not the only ones who were aware of it. "Although we did not discuss the Presence with many of our friends—just the one who gave us the quartz ball, to my knowledge—the subject came up at a gathering with friends, soon after our house went on the market. We happened to mention that we thought the Presence was unhappy with our decision to move. Since one of the people present was a person with whom I was sure we had not discussed our 'haunting,' I turned to explain to her what I meant by 'the Presence.' The friend immediately piped up with, 'You mean the one in your living room? Why do you think I never spent any time in there?'"

Whatever the being was that Catherine, Jeff and Alex lived with for so long, it must have been associated with the house and not with the family. Catherine is convinced that the Presence resided in the house long before she and her family got there. Because it has not followed the threesome to their current dwelling, they presume that the Presence has remained, unseen and unheard, in the living room of their first home.

The Castle

Given its long and colorful history, no one should be surprised to learn that there is at least one haunted house in Seattle's historic Georgetown district.

The particular house to which I refer is a very large, old building with many spooky tales surrounding it. Construction on the mansion began in either the late 1890s or the early 1900s. The enormous home was described by one person as being "a rambling structure ... complete with attic, basement, tower, [and] gables."

By the mid-1970s, however, the structure was not only haunted but badly dilapidated. The residence had been vacant for a decade by that time, and those years of abandonment had not been kind. The glass in most of the windows had been shattered, the porch was sinking in on itself, and the yard was a tangle of weeds and dead leaves. All in all, the property was a depressing prospect as a real estate investment.

Despite its terrible condition, an art dealer, whom we shall call Edward, was drawn to the house from the moment he first laid eyes on it. Just days later, he bought the building in a flurry of ambitious plans to restore the place to its original splendor. To complete the restoration in the most efficient manner possible, Edward decided that he must live in the house while he worked on it. And Edward lived alone.

As he settled into bed, preparing to enjoy the first night in his "new" house, Edward was only slightly unnerved by all of the noises he heard around him. He was more than happy to write those creaking sounds off as being the types of "settling" noises that such an old structure would naturally make.

But when he heard a woman's voice—crying "no, no, no"—he knew that he was dealing with something less "natural" than supernatural. This conclusion was confirmed by the sudden drop in temperature that accompanied the wailing.

Shivering with cold and fear, the poor man listened in horror to the sounds of a vicious brawl that seemed to be occurring directly above his bedroom. Again and again, he heard the woman's voice cry out as loud thumps shook the ceiling over his head. He was certain that a terrible fight was taking place one floor up from the bed where he lay. He was equally sure, however, that he was alone in the house. As Edward tried to align the two conflicting realities in his mind, the sounds of struggle reached a crescendo. Then, for no apparent reason, the dreadful noise abruptly stopped. For a few seconds, all was silent. Then Edward began to hear the sounds of heartbroken—and heartbreaking—weeping. Eventually, even those quiet whimpers ceased and his home was once again peaceful. Comfort and warmth had returned to the room at the precise moment when the sounds had stopped.

Edward fell into a fitful sleep for the rest of the night. In the morning he decided that the whole experience had been the product of his overactive imagination. To support this conclusion, the man somewhat nervously made his way upstairs. Upon opening the door to the room above his, what the man saw confirmed his initial assessment—there was a lot of work that needed to be done to the place, but there was nothing to indicate that anyone had been in the room recently. Certainly there were no indications of the terrible struggle that Edward had thought he'd overheard just hours before.

Edward tried to put the previous night's ordeal out of his mind during the day and, for the most part, he was able to do just that. He kept busy cleaning and repairing what he hoped would once again be a charming and attractive home. As night fell, he began to feel uneasy. Rather than spending a relaxing evening enjoying a sense of accomplishment, Edward kept pushing himself until he was too exhausted to work any longer.

It was nearly midnight when the man slipped into bed, certain that he would fall asleep immediately. But as soon as his head hit the pillow, the piteous wailing noises began again. His bedroom suddenly became icy cold and he was once again listening to the sounds of a life and death struggle, followed by terrible weeping and moaning. This time the crying seemed to come from all over the house. Choking back panic and the urge to flee, Edward let his heart and mind go out to whatever was causing the disturbance in his house. Initially, he doubted his own sanity. But once he had calmed himself sufficiently, the man realized that he was listening to phantom sounds—ghostly remnants of an awful struggle that had occurred in this house many, many years before.

Determined to discover what terrible incident had caused the house to become so dreadfully haunted, he began to investigate its history. It seems that the previous owners vacated the place because they could no longer stand living with the floor-rattling racket that filled the house every night. At least Edward now knew that he was neither losing his mind nor imagining things, so he took his research to another level.

It was then that the art dealer learned the truth. The phantom fight was believed to have been taking place in the house, whether it was empty or occupied, every night since at least 1910. Rather than making Edward more frightened about staying in the house, this information made him all the more determined to get to the bottom of the story—and to remain in his new home. Using archival newspaper stories, the homeowner finally put together the last pieces of the puzzle.

Early in its history, the enormous house had served for a time as a brothel. At 12:30 AM, in a room on the third floor, a young prostitute had been beaten to death by her lover, Manny. The house had apparently been haunted ever since, hosting a spectral recreation of the ghastly crime night after night.

Variations on this ghost story describe a female apparition with "eyes that burned like coal" wearing a long, white flowing gown and grabbing at her own throat. Some think the ghost is the spirit of Sarah, the granddaughter of the man who built the house.

Perhaps the positive energy that Edward brought to the haunted house has, by now, created peace for all of the old mansion's inhabitants—the living and the dead.

Sam Lives Here

They always referred to the spirits in their very haunted house by the single moniker "Sam." Even so, the family had seen ample proof that their home was haunted by far more than just one ghost.

Try as I might, I could not learn the true identity of this family, who lived in the Seattle suburb of Kirkland more than 35 years ago. At the time the haunting was active, however, the facts of the case were carefully documented by journalist Don Duncan of the *Seattle Times*.

For our purposes here, we shall call the afflicted family the MacMillans. Their adventures with the supernatural began in 1962, shortly after they moved into their new home. Mr. MacMillan, a successful businessman who prided himself on his astute dealings, was extremely pleased with the final price he had paid for the large, luxurious and almost-new split-level home. Little did he know at the time that he and his family were to end up with far more than they had bargained for.

Signs of the haunting surfaced not long after the empty moving truck had driven away. Billiard balls on the family's pool table in the gameroom began to mysteriously move about on the felt surface when no one was near them. Other games, those powered by electricity, operated in short bursts when they were not turned on, and MacMillan reported that furniture "rearranged itself."

At first, because they were new to the house, no one in the family said a word to anyone else about the strange goings-on that, by now, each family member had noticed. It wasn't until Mr. MacMillan asked what he thought was an innocent question that any such discussions began. As he arrived home from work one afternoon, MacMillan glanced at the house from his car and was surprised to see an elderly couple standing in his living room, looking out the window toward the street. He knew he had never seen these people before, and even stranger than their presence in his home was the way they were dressed. They wore, the man later explained, "very old-fashioned" clothing.

Curious, MacMillan parked his car in the garage and made his way into the house. Because he was certain that his wife was entertaining guests in the living room, he was astonished to find her working in the kitchen, preparing the family meal as usual.

"Where's our company?" he inquired.

"Company?" Mrs. MacMillan assured her husband that there was no one in the house but the two of them. To make absolutely sure that strangers had not somehow gained access to their home, the couple carefully searched the place from top to bottom.

"I think we need to talk," Mr. MacMillan declared when they were through. His statement finally paved the way for a long overdue conversation.

Moving furniture, moving billiard balls, electric games that would clang and bang even when there was no power nor anyone near them—they both admitted that they had noticed these things. Then there were the apparitions that Mr. MacMillan had seen so clearly today. What was happening here?

"I don't know," Mrs. MacMillan replied. "But I do know who it was you saw in our living room."

"You do? Then why didn't you tell me before. Who are they?" the woman's husband demanded.

Mrs. MacMillan explained that while she didn't know the couple's identity, she was somewhat familiar with their presence because she had recently watched in shocked amazement as two men, dressed in clothes from a previous era, appeared from within a closet, walked along the hall and disappeared again into a bedroom.

After well over an hour's discussion, the couple came to no conclusion except to agree that they would keep the knowledge of their strange surroundings a complete secret. No one, not even their children, must know. They did not want to be seen as "odd" in the eyes of their peers in the community.

Several weeks later, the MacMillan's daughter, whom we shall call Susan, came home from college for Christmas vacation. One evening the girl was curled up with a novel in front of a roaring blaze in the fireplace. Her parents were going out for dinner. They had invited their daughter to join them, but Susan had chosen to stay home and relax. For this reason, the MacMillans made it a point not to be away for very long. Even so, they returned to discover that they were too late. Their daughter met them at the door, already packed to return to college. It took nearly an hour of parental prodding and reassurance to convince the girl to tell them what had upset her so.

It seems that as Susan was enjoying her book, a movement in the room caught her peripheral vision. She looked up and was horrified to see a strange man in the house. Worse, this man was not any kind of "normal" intruder, for he had walked out of a closet—by passing right through a closed door! Like the men her mother had seen a few weeks earlier, this phantom walked down the hall and into the bathroom before vanishing. The girl had been convinced herself that the manifestation had been caused by remnants of the exam stress she had suffered while away at school. She did not want her parents to worry about her mental health, so she had decided that it would be best if she returned to her dorm immediately.

Although it must not have been much of a consolation, the MacMillans were able to assure the frantic young woman that, while she was fine, the family home was undoubtedly haunted.

As winter gave way to spring, the haunting moved outside the house for the first time. For example, croquet mallets left in one place would be found in another.

"Sometimes you get the idea that 'they' are just pulling your leg and having fun," Mr. MacMillan revealed. "At other times, it seems 'they' are angry."

The situation in the big, beautiful haunted house came to a head when Mrs. MacMillan ran screaming from the couple's bedroom. Mr. MacMillan ran to her side as quickly as he could, but found his wife incoherent. He accompanied his wife back into their bedroom, but all she could do was point to their bed. The man could hardly believe his eyes —but he could certainly understand his wife's horror. There, on the bedspread, was the indented shape of a reclining human body. As they both watched, the indentation moved and changed shape—"as if someone was sitting up."

Oddly, rather than prompting the MacMillans to immediately put their house on the market, that particular incident led only to their naming the household phenomena "Sam." They also began to research the home's short history. While they were never able to account for the ghosts, they did discover that the first owner had lived in the house for just a few months. Next was a young couple to whom the first owner rented the house on a short six-month lease—but the couple did not manage to stay in the house even that long. The MacMillans could certainly guess the reasons that none of the previous occupants had stayed any longer. Moreover, Mr. MacMillan began to suspect that the excellent deal he had negotiated on their home had been the result of the seller's desperation, not his own well-honed business abilities.

From that point on, the living came to something of an understanding about the dead occupants of the haunted house. Realizing that the ghosts were truly in a world of their own, seemingly unaware of anything taking place in the present day, the family began to make an effort to ignore the entities. After all, the ghosts were certainly not going to harm anyone. They were merely carrying on their own lives—or, perhaps more correctly, their afterlives.

Mr. MacMillan did admit that it was unnerving to know that he was the only one at home while listening to water running behind a closed bathroom door. Worse, however, was hearing the taps shut off, watching the door open, and seeing no one there.

At last report, the haunting was still active. Because Mr. and Mrs. MacMillan would be quite elderly by now, it is doubtful that they still live in the haunted house in Kirkland. However, if anyone reading this book is contemplating buying an apparent real estate bargain, you might do well to carefully check the house's history before signing on the dotted line. Most folks could probably not adapt to living in a haunted house as well as the MacMillans did back in the 1960s.

Haunted Prize Winner

According to an article in the *Spokesman-Review*, an award-winning historic house in Spokane was thought to have been home to a ghost. Perhaps because the old Marr House had been left to deteriorate for so many years, it had developed a reputation for being haunted. Once the current owners began the restoration work that would eventually win them civic recognition, the place no longer looked nearly as spooky as it had. Despite the vastly improved appearance of the home, the owner made comments to a journalist which seemed to indicate that this was not a ordinary house, but one that had a mind of its own.

During the refurbishing process, the woman explained, the goal had been to restore the building to what the house itself wanted to be. One clear indication of a preference they were given had to do with color. When it came time to choose shades of paint, the owners got a strong indication that the "house hates white." The couple acquiesced to the house's wishes, so it would seem that, in this case, history is being well cared for.

House Haunter

The year was 1918 and the world's population rejoiced in celebration. The terrible carnage that was the "war to end all wars"
had finally ended. For a time it seemed that people could back get
to the business of living. Tragically, what should have been was not
to be. The decimation of the population continued. A dreadful
epidemic of influenza, one that would leave few North American
families intact, was spreading with lethal strength and speed. Once
the deadly virus set out on its course of destruction, there was
nothing that could be done to stop it; little could be done even to
control its deadly rampage.

The tragedy and human suffering caused by the 1918 flu epidemic would, before it was over, rival that of the war; its victims,
however, were chosen even more randomly. It was not just soldiers
who were dying. No one, young or old, male or female, was safe
from the disease's virulent ravages.

Fritz Lee, of Shaw Island, was one of the fatalities. As best we can
reconstruct from the scant information that has survived, Fritz was,
before contacting the virus, a healthy 21 years old and a much-loved
son. Neither of those facts, however, could protect him. Before he
had celebrated his 22nd birthday, Fritz Lee was dead.

With heavy hearts, Fritz's parents buried their son just a few
yards from their home at Blind Bay. Then, as best they were able,
the Lees tried to get on with their lives. Nearly 40 years later, Al
and Lotte Wilding, the Blind Bay property's new owners, found
tangible proof of that terrible burden. They discovered a collection of Fritz's letters to his mother and his old school books
stashed away in the house.

The discovery must have been an enlightening one. When they
bought the place, the Wildings had no idea they were acquiring

anything more than a recreational property. It wasn't until later that they realized they had taken over property possessed by a ghost—a ghost they came to think of as "their gentle spirit."

Fritz was always very accepting of—probably even fond of—both Al and Lotte Wilding. His spirit never directly gave the Wildings any trouble. It was only the couple's guests who were occasionally startled by the resident ghost.

Al's uncle was the first to experience Fritz's presence. While staying overnight during a visit with the Wildings, the uncle was sleeping in what had been Fritz's bedroom—the very room in which the young man had died—when he woke with a start. The disoriented man was certain that there was someone standing near him, watching. Al's uncle opened his eyes to see who had come in to the room, but he found himself alone. Only mildly concerned about the experience, the man simply rolled over and went back to sleep. A few hours later, however, the same thing happened. Again, the man woke up with the impression that someone was in the room with him. Again, he checked to see who might have come in, and again he found the room empty. He was sure, though, that another presence had been in the room—staring at him while he slept.

Despite the disturbed sleep, Al's uncle accepted the room for a second night. That stay, however, was his last. The next morning, he told his hosts what had been happening throughout the night and explained that he was no longer comfortable staying in the room. The Wildings were quick to accommodate their uncle's request for a change. They moved him to another room and, over time, the bedroom with the strange sense of an unseen presence was used less and less frequently as sleeping quarters; eventually it was used only for storage.

Unfortunately, that change didn't stop Fritz from disturbing the Wilding's guests. Two couples whom Al and Lotte had invited to the island reported hearing footsteps climbing the staircase and walking along an upstairs corridor. Afraid that a burglar had somehow broken in, they investigated immediately but found the entire second floor empty—empty of visible souls, that is.

The ghost was not always so passive. During another visitor's stay, Fritz was really quite intrusive. As the guests went about their day, they were listening to the radio. Or, more accurately, they were trying to listen to the radio. It was tuned to a station broadcasting rock and roll, but the guests soon noticed that they were not listening to lively music at all but rather to "easy listening" tunes. They checked the radio and discovered that the dial was no longer set to the station they had chosen. Slightly puzzled, they changed it back to the rock and roll station. Moments later, that same radio was once again transmitting the "softer" sounds of the station they had just tuned out. In exasperation, they stopped what they had been doing and moved the radio to the kitchen table so they could see it more clearly. As the guests watched, the radio once again began broadcasting from the unwanted "easy listening" station. The ghost evidently did not enjoy rock music.

The kitchen figured prominently in another display of ghostly hijinks. The Wilding's daughter, who did not live with her parents on the island, watched as pots and pans that had been hanging from hooks on the kitchen wall began to move from side to side with enough force to bang into each other. No one was visible near the utensils at the time.

Although Fritz never manifested as an apparition, his existence was hard to deny. In 1987, after owning the property for nearly 30 years, the Wildings decided to sell it. When advertising the sale, they were careful to specify that the house came with a "gentle resident spirit." In 1990, for undocumented reasons, the new owners employed a psychic to free Fritz's soul from this dimension and to guide it to eternal rest. Presumably the old house on Shaw Island is no longer haunted.

The Captain's House

The property and house at Gig Harbor meant everything to the sea captain. He had put his whole heart into building the big two-story home, and he eagerly anticipated the day he could retire from sailing to enjoy a more settled existence. Alas, that day never came—at least not while the captain was alive. On the voyage that proved to be his last, a piece of equipment fell from the vessel's mast, striking the sailor's head. The man's crew rushed him ashore to a hospital, but his injuries were massive and he never recovered. He died, never having enjoyed the house to which he had so looked forward to retiring.

Violet and Lyle Severtson and their family did not know any of this when, just at the end of World War II, they moved into the house that the captain had built. They only knew that they loved the home's idyllic setting on a scenic knoll, amid fruit trees with a view of the harbor. After only three months, they also knew that there was something extremely eerie about the place and that they could not remain in the house any longer. Two weeks later, Violet's sister, Ann, her husband, Chester, and their two little boys moved into the place. All was calm and peaceful until spring, when Ann heard footsteps on the floor upstairs. Because she was certain that she was the only one home, Ann immediately investigated. She found no one—and no way to account for the strange sounds. Convinced that her imagination was playing tricks on her, Ann returned to the main floor.

Once again, she clearly heard the sounds of footfalls coming from the second floor. Determined to catch the prankster, Ann darted for the stairs again. She planned to make her way upstairs as quietly as possible and to wait, in silence, on the second floor landing until the intruder came into view. As she reached that spot, however, the curtains from the window at the landing suddenly blew inward and surrounded her, spoiling her vantage point.

Making a mental note to close the window, Ann disentangled herself as quickly as possible. The moment she did, however, she realized that there was something abnormal going on in her house. The window was shut, so it could not have been a draft that caused the curtains to envelope her like that.

After thoroughly checking the upstairs of the house and assuring herself that no one was there, Ann went back down to the kitchen to finish her chores. All was quiet for the rest of the morning, but she heard the phantom footsteps again that afternoon. Again she investigated—and again she found the house as empty as it should have been.

Ann's concern about the situation was growing, but she did not relate the incidents to anyone else in the family. Not, that is, until her brother, his wife, and their two sons came to stay for the night. The little boys were to sleep in a room on the main floor of the house. The children settled in for the night without any problem, but in the middle of the night the two-year-old boy woke everyone in the house with his repeated screams of "that man, that man!"

All of the adults except the boy's Aunt Ann were convinced that the child had suffered a nightmare. Ann did wonder what the exact cause had been, because the child was very specific about having seen a man in the living room. Perhaps it had been the same "man" that she had heard walking around the house some weeks before. In an attempt to coax the boy back to sleep, the family tried to encourage their dog to keep the children company. Unfortunately, the usually obedient hound simply would not enter the room. The dog's hackles were raised, and it growled menacingly at something none of the people were able to see.

When their guests had gone, the McIntyre's life soon got back to normal—until the time their 11-year-old daughter woke in the middle of the night, screaming in terror. When Ann had her daughter calmed down enough to speak, the girl told a story almost identical to the one related by her young cousin some months before. A man had been standing in the room, the child maintained. Because Ann's daughter was older than her nephew, the girl was able to give a more complete description. She insisted that the man had been wearing a dark-colored pea jacket, the kind that sailors wear, and that his head was bandaged. She also reported that he had vanished as mysteriously as he had appeared.

The apparition was clearly gaining strength now. It was September when Ann herself saw the image. She too had been asleep when something woke her. As she opened her eyes, Ann realized she was not alone in the room. A man stood near the doorway, watching her sleep.

The startled woman yelled at the image, jumped out of bed, and ran to turn on the light switch. Once the glow from the fixture filled the room, Ann was alone again. This did nothing to calm her fears, however, because she realized that, in order to turn on the light, she had reached right through the image of the man—the image she now realized was a ghost.

Ann searched the entire house but could find no trace of the strange man she had seen in her room. The next morning she thoroughly checked for footprints outside, but found nothing. Ann now realized that she had to talk to her sister Violet. She needed to know why Violet's family had moved out so abruptly after living in the house for such a short time.

Ann called on Violet a few days later. Ann soon steered the conversation toward the strange presence in the house.

"You've seen him too, have you?" Violet replied.

Now Ann knew her suspicions had been correct—the house was definitely haunted. For reasons not related to the ghost, Ann

McIntyre's family moved on—but before they did, they found tenants for the big old house. If those occupants ever saw or heard anything out of the ordinary, they kept the experience confidential. However, the new occupants did tell the McIntyres that they had been visited by the widow and daughter of the sea captain who built the house. That was how Ann finally came to learn the identity of the ghost with whom she had shared her home. The original owner of the house had simply never left it.

Addition Brings Ghost

By the 1930s, the Mount Pleasant school district—located along Highway 14 near the town of Washougal—had abandoned its one-room school in favor of more modern digs. Such a move was hardly noteworthy when you consider that the small building had served the southwestern Washington community since 1892. What was perhaps surprising was the decision not to tear down the building. The old school was sold to a family who made the necessary changes to convert it into a residence before moving in and happily calling the place home. What is even more surprising is that the well-used building was not haunted—at the time. It wasn't until another house was moved onto the same lot to serve as an addition to the old school building that the family acquired a ghost.

The spirit certainly displayed a distinct personality. Although psychics assured the homeowners that the presence was with them year-round, he only drew attention to himself when they and their family celebrated holidays. During the Thanksgiving weekend of 1992, the owners' son-in-law was awakened in the night by a feeling of pressure on his chest. He sat up in bed with a start, his eyes opening wide in near-panic. Staring back at him, only inches away, was a disembodied set of eyes. Before the man could even scream in fright, the eyes turned away and vanished. He later realized that those had not been human eyes that held his gaze. They weren't animal-like, either, but they were most definitely not human.

Despite his experience that night, the man maintains that he is a skeptic. He insists with equal conviction that he will always sleep in another room when he stays with his in-laws.

Two years later, other relatives were staying at the haunted house. The gathering was again to celebrate Thanksgiving. This time the ghost visited a woman who was sleeping in the room directly below the area where the previous visitation had occurred. This guest also woke to the feeling that there was a weight on her chest. She described it as something walking lightly over her chest. Like the owner's son-in-law, she also saw a pair of eyes staring intently at her. In a tremendous display of spirited resolve, she ordered the ghost to leave. The eyes vanished immediately.

After hearing of the second, similar experience in that particular section of their home, the owners decided that they needed to talk to the people from whom they had bought the house. Despite a concerted effort on the part of the homeowners, they were never able to track the couple down.

The Spirit's Gone

Because I have not been able to personally contact the residents of this haunted house, I have chosen to use pseudonyms throughout the following ghost story.

From the moment they moved into the house in 1968—and for the next 10 years—Pat and her middle-aged daughter, Diane, shared their Tacoma home with a phantom. The first ghostly encounter occurred when the doorbell rang emphatically at 4 AM. Hearing loud noises in the dead of night can be a disturbing enough experience for anyone, but the fact that there was no doorbell in the house made the women's experience even more frightening. It also set the stage for what was to come. Phantom knocks and scratching sounds at the door soon became almost routine.

The master bedroom was of a good size, but Pat found she couldn't sleep in it. "The light in the walk-in closet would switch on and off by itself in the middle of the night," she recalled.

On one occasion Pat was so convinced there was a real live intruder in her home that she called the police. She told them that she had seen the intruder's shadow on the basement wall as she looked down the stairs. The police searched the entire house, but did not find anyone or anything that shouldn't have been there. Such official word did not bring Pat much comfort. Over the next few weeks, she watched assorted cups and the cast iron lid to a pot fly across her kitchen as though propelled by an invisible force. At least she was able to find those objects when they were done moving about; other items, kitchen towels for example, would disappear completely before turning up just as mysteriously some time later.

The ghost wasn't always a nuisance, however. When one family member locked himself out at night, the stranded man was afraid he was going to have to wake someone up to let him in. As it turned out, he merely knocked quietly once and the door opened. He walked in, ready to thank whomever had shown him this kindness, but there was no one there—and he found the rest of the family asleep in their beds.

Pat's bed figured prominently in one display of ghostly strength. While standing near her bed, Pat felt a small but strong hand push her. She fell onto the bed.

Signs of the haunting began to fade in the late 1970s. Pat and the other members of her family met this change with mixed emotions. While on the one hand they were relieved to be free of the spirits, on the other they realized that the ghost's presence in their home had made them feel protected and special. Despite the longevity of the haunting, no one could ever figure out for certain whose spirit had resided with the family in Tacoma.

Battle Ground Ghosts

At least two houses in Battle Ground, Washington—and a third one nearby—are haunted. The ghosts do not seem to be connected with one another.

The following story concerns a building that had been converted from a commercial building to a residential duplex. The first tenants to rent the space as a home were a single mother named Betty and her two daughters. The little family was delighted to find such an inviting place to lease. The monthly rent was low and both the building and the yard were spacious. Not long after moving in, the mother detected something very odd— initially she didn't suspect this abnormality had any paranormal connotations, but it was very odd just the same. She noticed that her daughters were extremely well-behaved whenever they were in the house. It was as though they felt someone was watching them, the woman remembered thinking. Whatever the cause, the result was something she enjoyed.

The family's only complaint about their new rental house was that they would occasionally hear strange and inexplicable noises in the basement. The mother also became annoyed that no matter how frequently she closed the door to the basement, it would not stay closed.

Betty never thought to connect the change in her daughters' behavior with either the door to the basement or the sounds she sometimes heard down there. Then one evening Betty found herself unnerved by her daughter Connie's peculiar movements while the child watched television. Every few minutes the girl would look behind the couch she was sitting on—and then extend her gaze up to the ceiling.

Puzzled, Betty asked her daughter what kept distracting her from the television show she was watching. Sounding surprised at her mother's question, the child answered in an absolutely matter-of-fact manner. "I'm watching the people walking from the basement into our upstairs," she replied. "Can't you see them?"

Children are often more able than adults to see the ghosts in their homes. Connie is now a grown woman, and she later recalled in an interview that she had been conscious of the spirits in the house right from the start. That was why she always behaved as though there was company when she was in the house. She frequently watched the path of the apparitions as they proceeded from the basement to the upstairs level of the family's home. One time she followed the specters—and was startled to find that they kept climbing even after they had reached the top stair.

Several months later, Betty learned what sort of business the building they were living in had been before it was converted to a duplex; it had been a funeral parlor. Connie wondered if the manifestations she had seen were the spirits of the dead departing this world. Whatever the explanation, Connie and her two well-behaved daughters enjoyed their stay in the haunted house.

Keep On Keeping On

Some ghosts seem to be present only because they do not realize that they are dead. These souls go about their familiar routines as though they were still living. The following story is also from Battle Ground and is most likely an example of souls not realizing that their time in this realm has ended.

The family routinely heard the front door of the house open, followed by the sound of footsteps making their way across the floor. One time those phantom noises were even followed by the rustle of pages, as though someone was reading the newspaper. The sounds were so clear that the woman of the house presumed that her husband had come home. When she went into the living room to join him, she was quite startled to see that the room was empty.

In typical haunted-house fashion, the family would frequently find that small objects went missing for a few days at a time. Indeed, they became used to this and took it in stride. But when the unseen entity lay down beside their daughter on her bed, they were not able to accept that event so calmly.

Some years later, that same daughter was attending a convention in Seattle when she struck up a conversation with a complete stranger. By strangest coincidence, the stranger had once lived in that same haunted house. Between the two of them they were able to confirm each other's experiences.

After further investigation, the family came to believe that they had learned the identity of their ghost. She was a teenager killed in a car accident. The girl had not led a happy life overall; the happiest times she had experienced had come while she was living in that house in Battle Ground. Once the family knew who the spirit was—and were certain that she meant them no harm—they happily accepted their unusual houseguest. Because this haunting seems to have the approval of all involved, it may go on for a very long time!

Memories Remain

Another haunted house near Battle Ground is gone now, but the memories it gave three people who were children during the 1970s will linger in the subconscious to haunt them forever.

The place appeared to be ordinary enough. It was a two-story home with the bedrooms on the upper floor. Roberta was a child of 10 when she, her sister, brother and parents moved into the house. Her sister would never sleep in the room assigned to her, complaining that it was always cold. Roberta didn't have the same gripe about her room, but she was extremely distressed by recurring nightmares.

The fact that the door to Roberta's clothes closet would never stay closed was not nearly as difficult for her to cope with as was trying to keep track of one particular doll in her collection. She'd find the toy in any number of different locations around the house, even though everyone in the family denied moving it. Worse, Roberta often had the feeling that the doll's eyes were following her—watching her.

When Roberta was 12, the family moved on, no doubt much to the children's relief. The next family had a teenage daughter and son. The daughter soon suffered nightmares identical to Roberta's. Another time, the young woman and her brother stood in the bedroom that was once Roberta's and watched in horror as a figure appeared from within the closet. They ran from the room in terror, and it was not until they were safely downstairs that either of them realized they must have run through the apparition in order to escape from the room.

Not long after that incident, the house burned to the ground. Because no one was injured in the blaze and the spirits seem to have left the property, the fire might be seen as having been a cleansing of sorts.

Enduring Entity

When Rick bought the house in the southwestern Washington town of Camas in the 1950s, he had no way of knowing that it was haunted. He only knew that the house had been the pride and joy of the first owner, who had built the little place over a number of years stretching from the late 1920s to the early 1930s.

The first sign that anything was amiss gave, in retrospect, a very good indication that the house was haunted. Electrical appliances would frequently malfunction, although all manner of investigation failed to turn up any problems. In frustration, Rick stripped out all of the original wiring and replaced it with new. Unfortunately, it appeared that he went to all that trouble for nothing, because the breakdowns not only continued but actually occurred more frequently. Rick could barely get the evening newspaper read without the light flicking off.

Appliances would function only intermittently, making cooking or even storing food a difficult chore. Rick eventually learned to accept the inconvenience and lived in the house for many years before he sold it to a commercial developer. The company tore down the old house, but even that did not stop the ghost. It is said that the business now standing on that site tends to have inexplicable electrical problems.

Haunted House on Wheels

In 1983 Kurt Nelson bought a double-wide mobile home in the southwest Washington town of La Center, and at first he was delighted with his purchase. Kurt was convinced that he had struck a very fine real estate deal. Little did he know that he had bought a lot more than he bargained for.

When tools he needed went missing, Kurt initially became annoyed. He soon found that the tools would eventually turn up again, just as mysteriously as they had disappeared. Conversely, when he tried to throw away an ordinary pen that had run out of ink, it kept reappearing on his desk. After this happened several times, Kurt lost patience, took the pen out into the yard, dug a hole and buried it. The next day, it was back on his desk.

Once when he was working outside, Kurt needed a particular shovel. He looked everywhere for it, even searching throughout the house. The shovel was nowhere to be found. As he was explaining to his son that the tool had been there one minute and gone the next, Kurt slapped his hand against the counter for emphasis. There on the counter was the shovel that had been missing.

One day Kurt walked into his kitchen and discovered that a bag of flour had been spilled on the floor. Instead of being scattered around the room in a mess, however, the white powder had been built up into the shape of a perfect pyramid. Soon after that incident, Kurt began to hear mysterious footsteps throughout the trailer. By now he knew for certain that the place was haunted— and so did his dog. The poor animal would not go inside, no matter how much coaxing Kurt gave him.

In one rather amusing episode, the clothes dryer began to work all by itself—no one had turned it on because it had been broken for quite some time. Nevertheless, the appliance was giving off a considerable amount of heat and the drum was rotating.

A neighbor of Kurt's who knew something of the paranormal performed a ceremony at the trailer. When, immediately afterward, the dog happily came into the trailer everyone knew that the ritual had been a success. So, unless you count the initial wear and tear on his nerves, it would seem that, in fact, Kurt did get a good buy on his trailer.

Man in the Closet

One of the strangest haunted house tales that I've ever come across occurred in Washington. Richland, in the south-central part of the state, was, for a time, home to a most amazing apparition. Not only was his appearance unusual but his actions were, too.

The first interaction between a family member and the ghost was not even recognized as a paranormal encounter for a full year after it had happened. The family's daughter, who was only three years old at the time, was suddenly able to do astonishing mathematical calculations. When the parents asked the little girl how she had learned to do this, the child informed them that "the man who comes out of my closet taught me." The parents assumed that she was imagining things and did not pursue the subject any further.

They might never have thought of the incident again if it had not been for the fact that the woman of the house actually saw the ghost. The specter was a tall man, wearing a western-style outfit. His first manifestation terrified the woman. One night she simply woke up to find a strange male standing beside her bed. Moments later, the ghost left the woman's room and headed down the hallway toward her children's bedrooms. It was only her concern for the children's safety that forced the terrified woman to follow. On the edge of panic, she followed the apparition as it entered her daughter's bedroom. Steadying herself to confront the man, she switched on the light in the child's room. There was no one in the room but her preschool-age daughter.

The next ghostly incident was stranger still. Once again the woman was awakened in the night—this time by the sound of the dresser in the bedroom being shaken. As soon as she opened her eyes, she knew that the ghost was in her room again. The apparition, however, was only visible from the waist down.

From then on, the family saw the phantom more and more often, usually just in the periphery of their vision. In an attempt to discover who the ghost might have been, the couple began to research the history of their house and the land on which it was situated. When they didn't turn up any clues, they wondered if the ghost had somehow been associated with one of their pieces of antique furniture.

Although the husband once invited the ghost to stay in their home, the otherworldly presence eventually proved too much for the wife to bear. The spirit would taunt her by imitating her children's voices and calling, "Mommy, Mommy, Mommy." One day, the pressure of living with this mocking presence simply became too much for her, and the woman screamed at the unwanted visitor, demanding that he leave.

Either the ghost didn't want to stay where he wasn't wanted or he was ready to leave anyway, for no one in the family has seen or heard him since.

Haunting License

Many of Washington's ghosts make their home on Officers' Row in Fort Vancouver. One of the buildings, now a private home, has a most distinct presence. In 1997, Mary, the occupant of the house, told reporters that she had known almost from the beginning that her home was haunted. In addition to the very distinct feeling of an unseen presence, lights and clocks around the place seemed to work on their own schedule—their own or a ghost's, that is.

The next sign Mary received was a lingering whiff of perfume from an invisible source. Then, finally, she actually saw the apparition—a hazy female shape. The ghost's features were defined enough that Mary knew she was being stared at. After a while, the image simply faded. Since that first manifestation, the ghostly woman has reappeared occasionally. But even when she doesn't see the ghost, Mary knows the spirit is still around. When she comes home after being away for several hours, she will find lights burning that had been carefully turned off before she left.

A Haunting Melody

Just outside Seattle, an entire housing project, the Duwamish Bend Project, was haunted by a phantom crooner. Beginning in 1949, the year the homes were built, occupants could hear wailing but were never able to track down its source. The unnerving cries continued for several years, and at some point began being accompanied by ghostly singing. Witnesses described "a deep, rich voice" belting out such popular tunes of the day as "Fools Rush In," "Blue Moon," and, of course, "Ghost Riders in the Sky."

Despite several energetic efforts to track down the source of the singing and to discover who the mysterious minstrel might have been, the strange performances remained a conundrum until they simply ceased during the mid-1950s.

Ghost in the Machine

The following bizarre events took place in Washington, but the information came to me from England. While that was certainly a convoluted route, at least the tale ended up where it belongs—in *Ghost Stories of Washington*. The people involved did not want to be identified, nor would they reveal specifically where their intriguing encounter took place. Fortunately for our purposes, neither omission detracts from this puzzling ghost story.

We do know that these incidents took place in a rural area of Washington and that the people involved had just become parents for the first time. The year was 1991. Peter and Sue (these names are pseudonyms) and their newborn son, Kyle, were living in a basement apartment in Sue's parents' home. All was going well until the cold and damp of winter set in. Increasingly, they all felt that the downstairs suite was just too cold for an infant's sleeping quarters. The couple made arrangements with Sue's parents so that Kyle could sleep upstairs, but in order to avoid disturbing the older couple, they bought a baby monitor. After setting up one monitor beside Kyle's cradle and one by their bed, Sue and Peter felt much more comfortable. Their little son would be warm and they would hear him if he needed attention during his rest.

The baby slept soundly through the next few nights. Sue and Peter were therefore somewhat startled when, about a week later, they were awakened by the distinct sounds of a baby crying. Sue raced up the stairs, hoping to reach her son before he disturbed her parents. As it turned out, she need not have worried. Her parents were still wide awake, sitting up watching television—and Kyle was enjoying a deep and silent sleep.

After checking on the child and having a quick conversation with her parents, Sue went back downstairs thinking she must have only dreamed about Kyle crying. What she found when she rejoined Peter in their bedroom did nothing to support that theory. Peter was sitting up in bed, looking worried. Beside him on the nightstand, the monitor blared with the sounds of a baby crying its heart out. Sue tried, as best she was able, to assure her husband that their son was fine and was not making any noise at all.

If this unsettling incident had occurred in an apartment building in a crowded city, the couple might have been able to convince themselves that their monitor was picking up another frequency. But they were deep in the country; the closest neighbor was "several miles away and in her late 60s," so that explanation did not hold up to scrutiny.

The strange cries returned more than a dozen times over the next few months. The pattern was always the same. Sue and Peter would be awakened in the middle of the night by anguished sounds transmitted over the baby monitor—not just any sound, but the distinct sound of an infant crying. They would rush upstairs only to find their child fast asleep.

In 1992, the little family moved out on their own to a place some 13 miles south of Sue's parents' home. They were looking forward to leaving the enigma behind. Unfortunately, during their first night in their new home, they were awakened by the familiar phantom cries.

One afternoon, when Kyle was about 18 months old, Sue and a friend were in the backyard doing a bit of gardening while the baby had his afternoon nap. Before leaving the house, Sue turned on the monitor beside the little boy's crib and clipped the receiver to her belt so she would hear the baby when he woke up. As the two women worked in the yard, the monitor began to transmit some disturbing signals.

Sue and her friend stared at one another in horror as they heard a strange woman's voice reciting, "This little piggy went to market. This little piggy stayed home. This little piggy had roast beef. This little piggy had none." As the voice spoke the last line of the well-loved children's game, "And this little piggy went wee-wee-wee all the way home," Sue's face drained of color. In the background she could clearly hear her son's distinctive giggle. Both women ran for the house and made their way to Kyle's bedroom.

"He was lying on his bed, sound asleep," Sue said. "The room was freezing cold, so I went to shut his window and pull up his blankets. As he turned in his bed and tucked his thumb in his mouth, Kyle muttered one word in his sleep—'Piggy.'"

That was the last straw as far as Sue was concerned. She'd had enough of the haunted baby monitor. She disconnected the transceiver by Kyle's bed, unclipped the receiver from her belt, and put the whole unit in the backyard storage shed.

Several months later, Peter and Sue decided to hold a garage sale to dispose of the many items from Kyle's infancy that they no longer used. The baby monitor was one of the first items they ticketed for the sale table. Because such devices, when they work properly, are undeniably handy for young parents, the monitor sold quickly—twice. Unfortunately, both times the gadget was sold, the people who had purchased it brought it back almost immediately, saying only that "it didn't work right." In desperation, Kyle's parents finally took the monitor outside and pounded it to bits with a hammer. That, they felt, was the only way they could be sure they were finally rid of the possessed baby monitor.

Century-old Haunting

The following ghost story is based on a report that appeared in the May 3, 1901 edition of the Dawson *Weekly News*. The events were reported in such detail that I felt completely secure in taking a bit of creative license in relating my version of the haunting.

During that long-ago spring, a house in Seattle was making international headlines. The little place, described as being "a four-room, single-door dwelling ... in the vicinity of Roy Street and 28th Avenue" was owned by the Gordon family. The excitement surrounding the house began on a morning when Mrs. Gordon and Rosie Ring, a 12-year-old girl who had been hired to help out with chores, were doing some housework. The older woman was trying hard to get back to her normal routine. Life had been difficult for her since receiving word just two weeks earlier that Tommy, her beloved younger brother, had died in a strange accident near his Alaska home. According to the newspaper report, "The manner of his death was not known ... nothing was known beyond the fact that someone had been told on good authority that he was dead."

And so it was that Mrs. Gordon found herself in a rather somber frame of mind when she first heard the eerie sounds. She asked Rosie, a normally quiet child, if the girl had made any noise.

"I was only scrubbing the floor," the child replied a little defensively.

"Did you hear anything?" the older woman persisted.

"Only a little knocking sound, ma'am. That's all I heard," Rosie replied.

"That's the sound I meant, child," Mrs. Gordon assured her. "You didn't make that noise?"

"No, ma'am. I didn't make it, but I did hear it. The knocks came from over there." Rosie identified the source by pointing across the room to a spot on the wall, near the floor.

"That's where I thought it came from, too," Mrs. Gordon muttered as she made her way to the part of the room that Rosie had indicated.

The pair listened closely and their attention was rewarded when more knocking sounds came from the wall. After a few moments, they looked at one another and smiled. The noise was coming from outside. It must be Mrs. Gordon's daughters playing tricks on them.

Mrs. Gordon put her finger to her lips and motioned for Rosie to draw near for a secret. "They should know better than to play games like this, especially now when they know my nerves aren't the best after Tommy's death," she whispered. "We'll catch them at their own game. Let's sneak outside, run up behind them and holler 'boo.' That'll teach them not to try to scare us—and besides, it will be the first fun we've had in days."

Barely able to stifle their giggles, the two quietly slipped out the door. Rounding the corner of the house and readying themselves to repay the Gordon children's practical joke in kind, Mrs. Gordon and Rosie Ring drew in their breaths. Just as they were about to yell 'boo' as loudly as they could, the pair stopped in their tracks. The little Gordon girls were nowhere to be seen.

"They must have run off already," Mrs. Gordon laughed. "We'll get them next time." The two went back in the house to resume their cleaning.

They were no sooner inside than the knocks started up again. This time Mrs. Gordon didn't find the "game" so amusing. She stormed outside, ready to reprimand her daughters for making nuisances of themselves. Rosie stayed inside this time and it was she, not Mrs. Gordon, who found the little girls. Both were lying quietly on their beds, the older one reading, the younger one sketching a picture of the doll she hoped would be her present on her upcoming birthday.

"The girls are in here," Rosie called out the window to Mrs. Gordon, who was angrily stomping around outside the house.

"Of course we're in here," the older daughter said. "We haven't moved from the bedroom since you and mother started the chores. Do you want us for something?"

"No, I guess not," Rosie replied, going back to her work.

Mrs. Gordon joined Rosie a moment later. Although she had a concerned look on her face, she said nothing. When the phantom knocks started up again a few minutes later, however, the woman decided that enough was enough. She didn't understand what was going on and she was frightened.

"Get the girls from their room, Rosie," Mrs. Gordon declared. "I don't think it's safe to stay here."

Confused and worried, the little group sought refuge at a neighbor's house until Mr. Gordon arrived home for the night.

"There's been knocking on the wall," Mrs. Gordon confided to her husband. "I don't know what's going on, but it's not natural."

"You and your superstitions," Mr. Gordon chuckled. "I'll go over and check for you, but I'm sure it was just your imagination."

Gordon was gone for nearly half an hour. When he returned to the neighbor's house where his wife and daughters waited, he was pale and clearly shaken. Gone was the confident swagger with which he had set out. Even so, he insisted that all was well and that everyone must go back home. "It was only the wind rattling the boards or something," he explained.

But just as the family settled in for the evening, the knocking resumed. Badly upset by whatever was causing the disturbance, Mr. Gordon picked up a lantern and went outside to catch what he sincerely hoped was a practical joker at work. The expression on the man's face when he stepped back into the house revealed that he had not found the cause of the trouble. Worse, his exploratory expedition confirmed what he had suspected after his first inspection. Whatever was making the sounds could not be seen—and was therefore not of this realm.

"The house is haunted, isn't it?" Mrs. Gordon asked quietly, so that their daughters would not hear.

Mr. Gordon's only reply was to nod gravely. The family spent a sleepless night listening to the noises, and in the morning they went to solicit the help of a neighbor who was known for her skills as a clairvoyant.

Seeing how upset the normally level-headed Mr. Gordon was, the sensitive woman dropped what she had been doing and followed the man back to his home. By now the knocking had grown so loud that it could be heard on the street some distance from the house.

As soon as the medium entered the haunted house, she slipped into a trance. Then, as the family watched, she began paddling with her hands at the air above her head.

"You'd think she was drowning," Mr. Gordon whispered, so as not to break the clairvoyant's trance.

"Oh, my heavens," Mrs. Gordon uttered. "It's Tommy, trying to get a message to us. He must have drowned."

As soon as the clairvoyant came out of her trance, she and the Gordons devised a method of communicating with the young man's tortured spirit. It was agreed that Mrs. Gordon would slowly recite the alphabet, and they asked the spirit to knock twice when she came to the letter at which he wanted her to stop. The method would be slow, but at least this way Tommy's ghost could spell out the message he wanted to get to his sister.

Over an hour later, according to an article in the *Weekly News*, the Gordon family understood the deceased's final wishes. "I want you to pray for me," the noisy presence requested. He also confirmed that he had drowned in an Alaskan river. Then, as suddenly as they had started, the noises stopped. Just as they did, the clairvoyant came out of her trance. Even Mr. Gordon later admitted that the house somehow felt different after Tommy's request. Perhaps the air was lighter, he thought.

Relieved, the family set about easing the distress that the deceased young man's soul was obviously experiencing. Throughout the balance of the evening and again the next morning, they prayed for Tommy. By the following afternoon, everyone was considerably more relaxed than they had been at any time since the episodes of phantom knocking had begun.

Much to their dismay, however, the racket began again that evening. This time the family didn't bother to bring in the psychic, but merely began responding to the knocks as they had the night before. Tommy's soul must have appreciated his sister's and brother-in-law's kindness, because this time he had a confidence to share with them. Painstakingly, the brother and sister communicated back and forth in the only way they could. After quite some time, Tommy was finally able to make Mrs. Gordon understand the detailed directions he needed to give her. They were directions to a gold mine that he had discovered and was now leaving to his sister.

That was the last time Tommy's ghost was ever heard or felt in the little Seattle house. After assuring himself that his sister would be able to find the fortune he had discovered, the young man's spirit went on to its final reward.

Ghost of a Chance

Even as they were moving into their "new" 1907-era house in Spokane, the Drake family was hearing rumors from the neighbors about ghosts.

"The children who had previously lived in the house wouldn't sleep upstairs because they saw strange lights," Judy Drake reported, while acknowledging that she had sensed absolutely nothing unusual about the place. Quite to the contrary, Judy found the house "friendly" and sensed that she and her family would be happy in it. This sense of calm seemed to have been enhanced over the two-month period that the Drakes had spent painting and decorating the place. They had certainly not noticed anything out of the ordinary.

By April 1970, the entire family was very much looking forward to moving in. When the movers finally drove away, everyone scrambled into the house to look around. In all the excitement, no one noticed that the family's cats were acting strangely. Because they were in a new place, the animals had been following the humans around quite closely—right up until the moment when the Drakes went down to the basement. The cats did not follow but stayed at the top of the stairs and watched. It wasn't until the Drakes were looking back on events, however, that they placed any importance on the cats' behavior.

The cats may have been aware of the resident spirit from that moment on, but Judy was the first human member of the Drake family to encounter him.

"I heard footsteps come up the basement stairs, move across the living room and walk into the den—through closed doors," she recalled. Although she could only hear the ghost, she is sure that her cats were able to see it, because they seemed to follow its route with their eyes. "Soon the footsteps sounded again as he came out of the den and returned to the basement."

Once again, the cats stopped dead in their tracks at the entrance to the basement staircase. The animals' behavior may have been consistent, but the ghost's wasn't. After climbing the stairs, the presence would often continue on into the Drake family's den; other times he would not. Judy Drake was, for the most part, accepting of the ghost's right to share the house—except that he had a nasty habit of unlocking the back door and leaving it open. Any suspicion that another member of her family might have been responsible for leaving the door ajar vanished the day Judy watched in silent amazement as an unseen hand disconnected the chain lock and pulled the door open. Aside from that one little nuisance, the Drakes and their ghost cohabited quite peacefully for more than a year.

In May of 1971, a sad and seemingly unrelated event occurred. Judy's beloved grandfather, an accomplished pianist, died. Exactly one month after the death, Judy was awakened in the night by the sound of the piano being played. Convinced that one of the cats had made the sounds by walking across the keyboard, she got up to put the piano lid down so that her sleeping family wouldn't be disturbed again.

Judy was therefore quite surprised to find her pets curled up and fast asleep. She was so certain of what she had heard that she presumed an intruder was in the house and picked up a vase to use as a weapon. Thus armed, she made her way into the living room and across to the piano. No one was in the room. After thoroughly checking the whole house, Judy was convinced that no one except her own family members were inside. That was when it occurred to her that the tune might have been her grandfather's way of saying his final goodbyes.

Oddly, after the incident with the phantom music on that night in 1971, the resident ghost evidently left. From that day forward, the cats were perfectly willing to go down the basement stairs, the footsteps were never heard again, and the back door was never unexpectedly opened. Judy was not able to offer any explanation for this apparent coincidence. Perhaps the visit from Judy's grandfather prompted the other spirit to disappear. There is much about the spirit world that we mortals have yet to understand.

Chapter 2

THE SPIRIT'S INN

Hotels, motels, inns and restaurants often serve as homes away from home. It is therefore fitting that many of these establishments are also home to ghosts.

As the following stories demonstrate, these presences, like ghosts everywhere, can range from barely noticeable to horrifyingly conspicuous.

Manresa
Manifestations

"Palatial," "elegant," "luxurious"—those are just a few of the adjectives that, with great justification, have been used to describe the Port Townsend hotel known as Manresa Castle. Of course, "haunted" is another word that's frequently applied, because many people believe that two ghosts inhabit the more than 100-year-old building. To be fair, however, it should be noted that there are other people, some with intimate knowledge of the Castle, who insist that there is no validity to any of the spooky stories associated with the place and that such tales are only foolish rumors. Perhaps an examination of the facts that make up the hotel's history can help us to decide whether to believe all of the ghost stories, some of them, or none of them.

Charles Eisenbeis, Port Townsend's first mayor, built the 30-room, four-story mansion, which he called Eisenbeis Castle, as a home for his family and a monument to his considerable financial success. Eisenbeis had emigrated from Prussia in 1856. In 1865 he married fellow Prussian immigrant Elizabeth Berghauser. They had four children together before Elizabeth died in 1880. Two years later, the increasingly wealthy man married again. Eisenbeis fathered another four children with his second wife, Kate; he died in 1902 at the age of 70. His family continued to own the palatial estate until the late 1920s, when it was purchased by an order of Jesuit priests.

These new owners added 20 rooms to the former family home to make it more suitable for their intended purpose as a training facility for priests. They also renamed the place Manresa Hall in recognition of the area in Spain from which their founder, St. Ignatius, had been born. The priests occupied the enormous building until 1968, when they relocated to Seattle. From then until now, the building has seen three owners—and two ghosts.

In 1968, when Joshua and Dolly Norris bought the old place, it was seriously run down and considered to be a real estate "white elephant." However, the Norris couple was convinced that if the Castle were carefully restored, the once-proud building could be a spectacular inn. They were right. By 1973, after considerable effort and expense, first from the Norrises and then from subsequent owners Ron and Carol Smith, the ornate woodwork, exquisitely carved mantels and hand-printed wall coverings had been reclaimed. Manresa Castle, renamed to honor the building's two previous incarnations, had become a study in elegance.

Both the Norrises and the Smiths can be counted among those who disbelieve the ghost stories concerning the Castle. "There is no ghost," Dolly Norris once stated flatly. The Smiths, after 17 years in residency, echo her sentiment.

Even Roger O'Connor, the hotel's general manager since 1991, admits that he has "never experienced anything out of the ordinary." O'Connor does, however, offer a possible explanation: "Perhaps I am just not susceptible to this type of activity."

These opinions come from highly credible people with undeniably intimate and long-term knowledge of the place. There are others, however, who have made equally strong and compelling statements to the contrary, people who have also formed their impressions from personal experience and have come to the firm conclusion that Manresa Castle is haunted by a pair of ghosts, one male and one female.

The male presence is believed to be the ghost of an anguished priest who hanged himself in the attic when the building served as a Jesuit school and retreat. Film crews from the television show Sightings went to a great deal of trouble to dramatize the priest's demise. Interestingly, however, there is no record to prove that any such suicide ever occurred.

The female presence may have also ended her life by her own hand. Her name is Kate. Although some folks feel she is the former first lady of the Castle, others say that the Kate whose spirit wanders the haunted halls was a young English woman and that the identical name is merely a coincidence. The English Kate was staying at the Castle in 1921, waiting for her fiancé to join her, when she learned that he had been lost at sea. Crazed with grief, Kate threw herself to her death from an upstairs window. One version of the legend has it that shortly after her death, news reached the Castle indicating that her young man was, in fact, alive and well.

Reports attest that Kate's image can be seen at a window, both during the night and at dawn. She is apparently recognizable by her white gown and dark, flowing hair. It may also be Kate's spirit that some of the overnight guests at the hotel have sensed or her movements that they have detected. In addition to pronounced "feelings" of a presence when no one is visible, guests have reported finding dresser drawers inexplicably left open and personal possessions such as shoes moved—just a bit—by an unseen hand.

The third floor, especially Room 306, seems to be the center of Kate's ghostly realm. Management had so many reports of supernatural encounters there that they actually placed a logbook in the room and invited guests to record any unusual activity they might have experienced and their reactions to it.

The logbook is no longer left in the room because visitors occasionally became so unnerved while reading reports from previous guests that they asked to have their accommodation changed. When scanning through some of those notations, that reaction is easy to understand.

Many of those who have taken the time to write in the book refer to hearing "thumping sounds from upstairs … like someone was walking," even when they know that there is no one on

Two very different spirits haunt this historical Port Townsend hotel.

the floor above them. They also report detecting inexplicable odors—some pleasant, some not so pleasant. Other guests have been less specific, perhaps only because they were not able to capture with words the unfamiliar feelings provoked by being in a haunted room. For example, two women visiting overnight from Bremerton noted that the Castle is "a great place"—but added that "Room 306 is kind of weird."

The occupant of Room 306 on September 24, 1996, was staying at the Castle while her daughter underwent emergency surgery at nearby Jefferson General Hospital. She acknowledged that "even with all the worry ... we had a great time" although "the light kept going on and off." That guest was so convinced that one of the ghosts caused the disturbance that she closed by declaring, "We will be back to visit Kate again."

On November 29, 1997, the mother of a family from Texas expressed disappointment at not having met Kate more directly. "If we had known she was coming at midnight, we would have stayed up and waited for her arrival," she wrote. At least they got to hear Kate. "We heard singing coming from the bathroom. It was a women's voice singing a ghostly tune."

Understandably curious, the woman "got up to go to the bathroom and see who was in there. The door swung open eerily. There was a swish of cold air and a glowing light. Then all the lights came on." The author of the note and her family concluded, "It was either a ghost or the staff of the Castle has a strange way of entertaining their guests."

Either way, the writer did assure all who read her words that they'd had a wonderful time and would be sure to return.

On June 1, 1997, the occupants of Room 306 penned the following words: "As soon as the lights were turned out, odd sounds began—shuffling footsteps, branches breaking, wind blowing. A strange glow came from the painting on the wall. A ghostly figure seemed to materialize along the right path. It was a young girl who seemed to be signaling to us. We recognized her from the portrait in the lounge. She appeared to hover between the beds, lost and crying softly, and then she slowly vanished."

Toward the end of August that same summer, a family staying in Room 306 was treated to a special effect that they probably thought they would only see in the movies. "At 1:00 AM, blue waves of color spread across the ceiling in a circular motion."

Another couple experienced a considerably less enjoyable sensation. All night long they endured the sounds of moaning and bumping coming through the walls. They presumed that they were unwillingly eavesdropping on another couple's night of passion in the next room. The next morning, however, they discovered that they had been mistaken. The room next to them, the one from which all of the noises had originated, had been unoccupied the entire time.

One of the eeriest notations is also the most subtle. In the fall of 1997, someone who signed only as "K.K. from New Mexico" wrote, "Around 3 AM I felt the sheets tighten at my feet, the sensation one feels when another person sits down on the foot of the bed. The 'visitor' had the lightness of a cat."

The only residents of Room 306 to be utterly terrified by their encounter with one of the Manresa Castle spirits were two women who stayed there on October 22, 1989. One woman woke in the middle of the night to the sight of an outstretched arm extending from a hazy light which had formed at the end of her bed. Moments after the apparition faded, the startled woman lay in rapt stillness, listening to footsteps retreat down the empty corridor outside her room.

The priest's specter seems to be a darker presence than Kate's spirit. One Washington family makes a point to visit the Castle regularly. They always bring their Ouija board in an attempt to communicate with the long-deceased Jesuit. In a dramatic and intimate revelation, the family asked the priest, through the Ouija board, for some references in the Bible to explain his presence. He led them to Psalm 101, which reads in part, "A perverse nature shall be absent from thee." The group took this to mean that it was a perverse or evil aspect of the priest's being that had led him to kill himself.

Guests are not the only people who have detected the ghosts at Manresa Castle. Manager Jill Tomasi explains that "several of my maids won't ever clean on the third floor" after they heard a disembodied voice softly calling to them. Tomasi is quick to point out, though, that the, "rooms do get cleaned ... we have people who don't have any fears about that kind of thing."

Events experienced by Castle employee Jim Flitton have left him with no doubt that the old place is haunted. Jim has been associated with Manresa Castle since 1991, and the number of paranormal encounters he's had while at work have been enough to convince him. These experiences have ranged from very vague ones, such as "getting the heebie-jeebies when I'm alone here and it's quiet and all the lights are off," to incidents that are considerably more specific and dramatic.

"One night I was pulling the graveyard shift," Flitton recalls. "It was about 2 or 3 o'clock in the morning. When people quit coming in and out of the doors, I turned out all the lights in the library, which is right across from the front desk. I was just sitting here reading when I heard leaves rustling in the library. I was thinking, 'There's somebody in there,' so I got the flashlight and my remote telephone and I went into the library. We had a huge tree in there, in a big pot, and it had just slowly fallen over."

Watching something of that size lay itself down with a deliberate and controlled motion must have sent shivers up the poor man's spine. He couldn't have been completely surprised, however, because he has seen many other examples of supernatural activity and knows that some of the ghostly goings-on actually happen according to a schedule. For example, Flitton knows to expect that "at about 3:00 or 3:30 AM, you can hear noises. It sounds like people are upstairs moving furniture around. Even if the rooms are unoccupied, it still happens just about every week-end. I've gone outside and looked up at the windows to see if the lights are on, and they never are."

It was while tending bar that Nick Gale witnessed perhaps the most disturbing manifestation. "A customer's glass shattered in his hand," the bartender recalled. "I thought it was interesting but didn't pay it any particular heed until the same thing happened to me and I was the one holding the glass that inexplicably shat-tered into shards."

Like General Manager Roger O'Connor, Nick Gale acknowl-edges that "some people are more sensitive than others to these phenomenon." Unlike O'Connor, though, Gale seems to be one of those more sensitive people.

Tammi Headley was a confirmed skeptic until she worked as a housekeeper at the Castle. She now agrees that the place is haunted. She, too, has seen an ordinary drinking glass fly from her hand and shatter. She also has sympathy for guests who report their room becoming too warm overnight because she has wit-nessed heater fans that turn on of their own accord. Room 306 has also treated Tammi to a unique lighting display. She recalled that, even though the shades were pulled down, "two bright flashes of light came from the door."

Despite these unnerving incidents, the haunting hasn't fright-ened Tammi. She concluded, "I do think there's someone there. It's her home. She's not trying to hurt anyone."

During the summer of 1997, a new chef came to work at the Castle. While he was getting settled into the area, management invited him to live in the hotel. One night he was curious about the bright lights shining under the door to his room. He opened the door, looked out into the hallway—and found it dark and empty.

Nick Gale described a further oddity at the former Manresa Hall. "Every time I've gone up in the turret area itself, I just feel like I'm losing my equilibrium," he said. "I don't like it up there. I think there might be an energy vortex or something up there." This theory has since been confirmed by psychics investigating the Castle.

And there are other odd occurrences that can't be explained. Lights turn on and off for no apparent reason, pictures come off the walls when no one is near them, and the distinct sounds of a person entering the ladies room can be heard when no one is there.

During a Christmas party in 1996, the grandfather clock in the hotel's library chimed in the wee hours of the morning. It had never, in anyone's memory, chimed before—and it has never chimed since.

Finally, as Gale notes, "There's always the old 'you think you see something out of the corner of your eye and then you look and there's nothing there' syndrome."

Manresa Castle definitely has all the signs of a haunted building. But if, as many reliable people have attested, Manresa Castle is not haunted, then how can we account for all of the bizarre activity? The "Philip Experiment" (see my *Ontario Ghost Stories*, Edmonton: Lone Pine Publishing, 1998), which was conducted in Toronto, Canada, received international acclaim as groundbreaking research. Not only was it a remarkable paranormal study in its own right, but the results may provide some insight into enigmas like the one in Port Townsend.

The parapsychological experiment began when members of the Toronto Psychic Society were called in to investigate a haunted house. The investigators had been told of a suicide in the house, but when they saw a hanging apparition, they wondered if their own expectations had not played an important role in their sighting. They then decided to see if they could create an entity where none had previously existed.

The "Group of Eight," as the participants called themselves, set about conceiving an entirely fictitious personality and placing him in both an era and a place. They determined, completely arbitrarily, that he would have been an aristocratic Englishman in the mid-1600s named Philip. They further decreed that he had lived a tragic life. The Group then met regularly, meditating together in the hope that their manifestation would appear. Patterning the method of receiving otherworldly messages after that used in Victorian England, they placed in their midst a small table through which they hoped the ghost would communicate. Unlike the Victorian séances, the Group kept the room brightly lit and insisted that an impartial observer be present.

Eventually, the table began to vibrate. This, they suspected, was their first indication that a supernatural being was present. They informed the entity that they wished to ask it some questions. The force was to respond with one knock of the table leg on the floor for a "yes" answer and two knocks to indicate a negative reply.

After a few sessions like this, something uncanny happened. The table—or, if you prefer, the spirit of "Philip," communicating through the table—developed a distinct personality. When it was happy, the table would reply enthusiastically, actually moving energetically around the room. When it didn't want to answer a question, there were scratching sounds. If it wasn't sure of an answer, the reply would be a decidedly hesitant series of knocks.

These meetings continued over many months. All of the members of the original assembly attended whenever they could make time to do so. Inevitably, however, there were evenings when one or more of the Group of Eight found it necessary to be absent. Interestingly, the personality of "Philip" changed each time the composition of the group changed.

Occasionally Philip's antics were not confined to the table. He would turn lights on and off and move things about. As with the enigma at Manresa Castle, word of the Philip experiment leaked out and the media came swooping in. In stark contrast to the priest who would not make himself known to the Sightings crew,

"Philip" acted like a real ham when the Group of Eight took the table to a television studio for a taping.

One of the group's participants told me, "We had a really fun time with the cameramen, as they could not keep up with where the table was going." On other occasions the table (or Philip) chased after skeptical television personalities and even a room full of academics. The Group of Eight had simply willed a presence into being. They had created a ghost.

Is it possible that, as some maintain, that Manresa Castle was not haunted prior to its present ownership, but that it is legitimately haunted now? Could it be haunted by two spirits brought to "life" through the power of human thought and will? This theory may possibly explain the strongly contradictory opinions about the presence of both Kate's and the priest's ghosts. Nothing, however, seems likely to diminish the public interest stirred up by this reclaimed piece of Port Townsend history.

Spirits With Your Meal?

Some people wonder about the identity of the ghost haunting the E.R. Rogers Restaurant in Steilacoom, but Jim Girvan is not one of them.

"Every night when I leave here, and I'm here five or six nights a week, I lock up," Jim said. "And every time I say, 'Good night, Catherine. Have a good evening.'"

Obviously there's no doubt in this personable man's mind that the ghost with whom he shares his work space is that of Catherine Rogers. Catherine was the wife of the original home owner, Edwin R. Rogers, a wealthy merchant and seaman who built the impressive house in 1891. Unfortunately, the man's fortune collapsed less than three years later and the family was forced to move out of their grand home. Thereafter, the place changed hands frequently. The Bairs, who owned the now-haunted Bair Drug Store in Steilacoom (see page 93), bought the property in 1920, thinking that its 17 rooms would be ideal for a profitable boarding house. The place served that purpose until Mrs. Bair's death in the late 1940s. Then the former mansion sat empty until the 1960s, when plans were made to tear down the palatial home. Fortunately, wiser heads prevailed and the building was preserved.

Today, a few folks have been known to wonder if the female presence in the old Rogers home might be Hattie Bair. However, Catherine Rogers would have had a far greater emotional stake in the house, so it is more likely that the popular opinion is correct and Catherine is the ghost.

There can be no question that at least one presence in the restaurant is female, for she—or more accurately, parts of her—have been seen. She is usually not very active while the restaurant is open, but a man who had been enjoying a drink at the upstairs bar was most startled to see what he described as "a woman's foot in stockings" suddenly materialize at his eye level. The apparition moved upward before disappearing into the attic. The sight must have been an unnerving one, but its location was not a surprise to anyone who knew the house. That area is known to be a favorite of the ghost's. As Jim Girvan put it, "Sometimes people put stuff up there and then lock the attic—and the next day, the stuff's been moved."

The attic area was also implicated in what was, at the time, thought to be a break in. The police were called, and they arrived with a trained dog. The animal swept through the entire ground floor as he had done in dozens of previous searches. When nothing suspicious was found, the dog's handlers instructed the animal to continue his search upstairs in the attic. For the first time in its life, the expertly trained dog refused to obey a command. No amount of ordering or coaxing could persuade the animal to enter that area. The police officer finally gave up and searched the area himself. The attic was empty—or whatever was in there couldn't be detected by human eyes.

On another occasion, not long after Jim had arrived home from a long shift, he received a call from the security company responsible for the alarm system in the house.

"They told me that the alarm had been activated and [wanted to know] did I leave anyone in the building," he recalled. "I said, 'No, no one's in the building. If you want to talk to someone who is close by, you need to call the bookkeeper who lives down the street.' So they call her and she says, 'Well, it's probably the ghost' and goes back to sleep. They call her again and say, 'No, there really is something going on in the house.' So she gets down there and meets the police. The police go in with their guns drawn and flashlights blazing—and the police dog would not enter the building. They kept trying and trying, but it would not go in. So they searched the whole building and found nothing. They came back out, reset the alarm, locked up and left. The dog never would go into the building."

Another episode undermined Jim's composure on a considerably more personal level. "This must go back five or six years," he said. "While locking up at night, we turn off the lights in the house. Certain lights stay on, such as the safety lights. On this particular evening, we went to the back door and I hit the alarm code so the security system would activate. Because my car was parked out back, I exited through the rear door and locked it behind me. I got in the car, started it up, and all of the lights in the house came on—every single light in the house! I came back in, turned off the

For the most part, the employees at E.R. Rogers Mansion enjoy the presence of their ethereal workmate.

alarm, went to the phone, called the alarm company—and they say, 'No, there has not been an activation of any lights on in the building whatsoever.' I said, 'No, I'm telling you that every light in the house is on.' They repeat, 'No, there's no activation.' So, I went around and turned off every light in the house, from the attic all the way down to the basement. Then I hit the alarm again, locked up the building again, turned to leave—and the lights all come back on."

The frustration the man must have felt at the time was still evident in his voice while he was talking about the incident. He was careful to assure me that the house "is up to [the standards of the building] code. It's not like this is an old house that's not up to code."

At this point in his evening, Jim had already worked a full day. He knew there was no one in the house—at least no one corporeal who could have caused any harm to come to the old place. He stood by his car, staring at the well-lit house and declared, "Catherine, you must be having a party. I'm outta here."

There was one last kicker to that strange night. When Kristi Gourneau, the restaurant's bookkeeper, arrived at work the following day, she found all the lights turned off.

The staff of a local rug cleaning company has had much the same experience. The company had been contracted to go into the restaurant after closing and clean all of the carpets. The next day, the manager opened up and discovered that just one rug in one room had been cleaned. He called the company to ask what the problem was, and he was told that, while there would be no charge for what they had done, the workers would not be back—ever. They were convinced that the place was haunted, and informed the restaurant manager in no uncertain terms that they refused to go back in and were not even interested in discussing the situation.

Less dramatic encounters occur regularly. Staff members hear their names spoken—but no one has called them, and no one is nearby. Hostess Jennifer Laughlin remembers suddenly detecting the scent of perfume and sensing that she was not alone—at a time when she knew she was by herself in the building.

As is common with many spirits, Catherine interferes with all manner of electrical wiring and electronic appliances. She causes VCRs and speaker systems to malfunction, she plays with the lights around the house, she's credited with changing channels on the television when no one is visibly near the set. Some of the restaurant equipment has even been known to fail intermittently for no apparent reason. Candles will mysteriously fly off the tables and slam against the floor.

Most people feel that these pranks are the work of the resident female wraith, but there are also those who have seen Edwin's image sitting in a rocking chair and looking out a north-facing window. They say that no matter where in the house they put it the chair, it always turns up in front of that same window.

According to Jim Girvan, the haunting at Rogers Restaurant has something of a seasonal flavor. "Catherine's ghost seems to be most active around fall and winter time," he says. And it was at that time of year that Jim had his most amazing encounter with Catherine.

"One night I was sitting upstairs in the bar. There are two dining rooms upstairs and a couple of ottomans sitting out in the hallway. I was waiting for Cathy, one of the servers, to finish so we could lock up and leave. I was sitting on an ottoman in a hallway that leads down to the dining rooms. As I was sitting there, just thinking about nothing, I saw... well, I didn't see anybody walking—but I did see indentations, footsteps going across the carpet. The footsteps turned at the corner and went toward the women's room. They turned around and came back, then they went into the south dining room, which is where most of the strange activity has been in the last few years. So Cathy came up the stairs and said, 'What's wrong with you? You're as white as a ghost.' And I said, 'You won't believe what I've just seen.'"

Despite Jim's suspicion that his co-worker would not believe him, he told Cathy in great detail about the indentations forming in the carpet as though an invisible person had walked past. Cathy evidently did believe Jim. "She immediately got goosebumps," he said. "You could still see the footprints, the indentations in the carpet."

Understandably, the pair did not dally. As Jim put it, "We just hit the alarm and left."

There may be some debate as to whether the ghost in the building is the spirit of Catherine Rogers, but there can be no doubt that the E.R. Rogers Restaurant is, in fact, haunted.

Ghost To Go

Carey Dahl, of Victoria, British Columbia, Canada, first saw the ghostly image while she was dining in a Spokane restaurant. It's a good thing that Carey wasn't startled by the apparition. Although she didn't know it at the time, the phantom was to follow her all the way home.

I couldn't find a current listing for the restaurant Carey described, but she did say that it was housed in "an old converted mansion." As the young woman climbed the stairs on her way to the washroom, she caught a blurred glimpse of the specter in the corner of her eye. Fleeting as that encounter was, it was enough to convince Carey that the presence was a female.

Because Carey had experienced ghosts as a child, she was not frightened by the entity. She simply paused momentarily on the stairs to compose herself before continuing. And that was when she saw a portion of the apparition more clearly. This time, rather than rushing past her going up the steps, the movement of the piece of long, gray dress that Carey could see indicated that the phantom was serenely descending the stairs.

The young woman stood and watched as the fragmentary image made its way to the bottom of the stairs, then turned and disappeared. That disappearance seems to have reduced the ghostly population of Spokane by one; the very next day, in her home miles away, Carey Dahl saw the same ghost.

Old-fashioned Hospitality

During the summer of 1986, a couple named Porter was driving through Spokane, Washington. They were tired and hungry, but unfortunately they were also short of cash. Much to their delight, Mrs. Porter spotted something quite promising. Directly ahead was a motel-diner combination with a large sign out front advertising the special of the day: "Steak and Eggs—$3.85."

Almost giddy with relief and anticipation, Mr. Porter parked the car in the adjacent lot and the couple made their way across it to enjoy a hearty—and inexpensive—meal. As they walked past the sign that had caught Mrs. Porter's eye, they noticed that it was evidently a very old advertisement and worried that their food bill might, therefore, be higher than they had originally hoped. But that no longer mattered to the Porters. The anticipation of a delectable meal had wiped away any semblance of control that they had been maintaining over their remaining funds.

From the moment they opened the restaurant door, the Porters' senses were filled with the aroma of good, nourishing food. They settled into a booth and briefly looked around. The diner seemed to be every bit as old as the sign out front, but it obviously still had a loyal following because the place was crowded with patrons.

The couple glanced somewhat distractedly at the yellowed, greasy menus that lay on the table where they had seated themselves. None of the offerings tempted them away from their intentions of ordering the steak-and-eggs special. A waitress soon arrived to take their order. When the food was served a few minutes later, it was hot, filling and tasty.

Anxious to get back on the road, the Porters asked for their bill as soon as they had finished eating. Mr. Porter couldn't believe his eyes—the total charge for both meals was less than five dollars! A more careful look revealed that they had been charged the advertised price of $3.85 for one meal, but that the waitress had mistakenly charged just 85¢ for the second meal.

Wanting to be honest, and feeling that they would easily have eaten their money's worth even if the bill had been twice as high, Mr. Porter brought the mistake to the waitress's attention. The woman thanked the couple for their honesty and apologized for the inconvenience that she had caused. Furthermore, she explained that company policy dictated that whenever a server made an error, the customer left with a bargain. The total on the check would remain at less than five dollars.

Understandably impressed by their experience at the restaurant, the Porters picked up a brochure about the motel connected to the diner before heading back to their car and on toward their destination.

Not surprisingly, the couple frequently described their lucky experience to friends and acquaintances. One of the people to whom they told the story knew downtown Spokane well but, oddly, could not picture such a motel-diner combination anywhere near the location the Porters described. The couple recalled that the restaurant name—The Chuck Wagon—had been emblazoned across the menus. This added piece of information was of no help to the man—he had never heard of the place. Puzzled, the trio consulted a Spokane phone book but found no listing for a restaurant by that name anywhere in Spokane, let alone in the heart of the city. Upon further reflection, Mrs. Porter recalled the name printed on the brochure that she had picked up in the motel office. That name was one their friend recognized. There certainly was a motel with that name in downtown Spokane, but he was sure that there was no restaurant associated with it—unless it was a very recent addition.

Mrs. Porter pointed out that such a conclusion made no sense—the restaurant had been old, not new. Now completely dumbfounded by the seemingly contradictory pieces of information, the group decided that this puzzle would have to be explored further. They phoned the motel and asked if there was a diner attached to it. The reply was both quick and sure, but it succeeded only in further baffling the trio. There was currently no restaurant at that location. Yes, there had been a diner on that spot—The Chuck Wagon by name—but it had burned down many, many years before the Porters visited Spokane.

The Porters' hunger had led them on a journey back through time—to an inexpensive phantom eatery, staffed by understanding ghosts.

Pharmacy Phantom

W.L. "Cub" Bair may have finally left work. Considering that he had been there since 1895, no one begrudges Cub his time off. Nonetheless, the employees in the Old Bair Drug Store at Steilacoom do miss his presence, even though Cub—or more accurately, Cub's ghost—could be a real nuisance at times.

The Steilacoom Historical Society restored the former drug store to house a popular restaurant and museum displaying, among other things, old medicine bottles, wooden mailboxes and even the original soda fountain. It's no wonder that the ghost of the former owner felt right at home. But all of the new equipment must have confused Cub, because he has been known to burn cinnamon buns to a crisp and to cause mixers and dishwashers to malfunction.

When it came to making an old-fashioned ice cream treat, though, Cub liked to keep his hand in. An employee who was getting ready to make a sundae was called away. There was no one in the kitchen at the time, but when he returned he found that the whipped cream had already been put on top of the ice cream.

The entity also liked to draw attention to itself. One evening, as several employees watched, all four coffee pots began to spin madly. Because the pots had just been washed and set back on the coffee maker, one employee reasoned that the strange motion might have been the result of the wet pot bottoms reacting with the machine's hot elements. The thought was a good one, but not applicable in this case—not only were the pots dry, but the elements were cold.

Cub's ghost demonstrated an apparent aversion to a product that the staff had hoped to sell in the store—bottles of a particular kind of sauce. While employees watched, these bottles would fly across the room and smash onto the floor. Store manager Rosa Kreger once watched the strange sight and confirmed, "That bottle didn't fall—it flew."

Cub's activities at the Drug Store have now apparently come to an end. "We renovated recently, and since then he seems to have left," explained an employee named Jeannie. "He might have gone to the bank next door, because their phones have started to act funny. The lines will ring and there's no one there, that sort of thing."

Cub Bair stands in front of his drug store circa 1900. Now he haunts the place.

Perhaps, if the long-deceased Mr. Bair has only "gone to the bank," he may still return to his old haunt before long.

Bair Drug today. The ghost of Cub Bair still minds the store and makes the occasional ice cream sundae.

Full of Life, Even in Death

When I phoned to investigate the well-documented haunting at the Rosario Resort on Orcas Island in Washington's East Sound, a young man named Nathan assured me that the resident ghost was still very much with them. To attest to this, he described a recent manifestation. "She knocked books off the shelves while I was locking up the Music Room," he said.

Such activity is really not much of a surprise for those familiar with this particular ghost. When she was alive, Alice Rheem was certainly a high-spirited woman. In 1938, her husband built a large home on the island as a last-ditch attempt at controlling Alice's wild ways. He must have hoped that virtually holding her captive on the island would slow her down somewhat. The man had clearly underestimated his wife's determination, because she immediately resumed her wild ways whenever he traveled away from home. The couple's neighbors on the island learned to expect some strange sights when Mr. Rheem was off conducting his business affairs.

Alice could accurately have been described as a "party girl." She liked the attention of handsome young men and she liked to drink. Alice herself would probably not have ranked those two pleasures in that order. Be that as it may, once she had imbibed sufficiently, Alice frequently rode her motor scooter around the island in search of a bit of fun. The fact that she would occasionally forget to put on proper clothing before taking these rides no doubt helped her find the fun she was craving.

Despite his best efforts, Mr. Rheem's attempts to confine his wife were never successful and the woman died prematurely of problems caused by overindulgence in alcohol. But as many people, including Rosario Resort employee Nathan, can attest, her spirit lives on.

In the mid-1980s, a housekeeper at the resort was too tired to make the drive home. Instead, she settled in an empty room for the night. The woman lasted in the room until midnight, when sourceless shadows and invisible fingers touching her hands drove the housekeeper out. The room she was staying in had been Alice's.

Members of a band who were assigned the room next door to Alice's complained about the noisy woman in the adjacent suite. She had been partying all night long, they protested. Management would certainly have done something about the situation if they could have. But the room in question had not been rented out. Because it had been empty all night, there was really little they could do other than try to explain that "Alice doesn't (really) live here anymore."

The Wandering Widow

In the early 1900s, Isadore St. Martin built a hotel at Carson, Washington, in the extreme south of the state, atop a natural hot spring. The business was something of a retirement project for St. Martin, as he had already enjoyed a varied career spanning nearly 50 years and had raised 10 children with his wife.

St. Martin firmly believed in the curative powers of the hot spring waters, and he not only wanted to have them available for himself and his wife but also to make them accessible to others. Building and operating a hotel at the site seemed an ideal way to combine the two aims.

Unfortunately, an elderly neighbor named Robert Brown did not share St. Martin's belief. In a heated argument, which escalated into a physical fight, Brown fatally stabbed the innkeeper. Brown was presumably punished for his crime, but it was St. Martin's widow who suffered the most. She died of a broken heart not long after her husband was murdered. The Widow St. Martin is believed to be the spirit roaming the hotel's hallways.

The ghost has only rarely been known to cause trouble. Once, when a maid was trying to make a guest's bed, she kept finding her work mysteriously undone. The woman put clean sheets on the bed and left the room to get the necessary pillows. Although she was gone only a moment and no one else entered the room in her absence, she returned to find that the sheets were not only off the bed but missing from the room entirely.

The maid went back to the supply cupboard and picked up a second set of sheets. After putting those on the bed, she left the room for a few minutes. When she returned, the second set of sheets was also missing. No doubt feeling rather exasperated, the woman retrieved a third set of sheets from the linen storage. Once again she fitted them neatly to the bed, and this time they stayed in place. The incident has been blamed on the ghost of Mrs. St. Martin, who was apparently always very fussy about the way the guests' rooms were made up.

On another occasion, the ghostly widow must have been rather annoyed with a particular maid. When the unsuspecting woman was making up a room, the pillows suddenly flew straight at her.

The third floor of the hotel is no longer used—by anyone living, that is. Although the entire floor is empty and access is closed off, footsteps are frequently heard in the abandoned area.

The long-dead woman's image has even been seen a few times—strolling through the lobby, inspecting the guestrooms or simply walking along a hallway.

Despite his violent and sudden death, Isadore St. Martin appears to have gone on to his eternal rest. No one has ever mentioned a ghostly male presence in the old hotel.

Royally Haunted

When it was built in 1910, the Palace Hotel in the Yakima Valley town of Prosser lived up to its regal name. The next 75 years, however, were not kind to the place. By 1985, when the owners began massive renovations, the hotel was badly deteriorated. Today, the building is a bed and breakfast and is once again a point of civic pride. In spite of all the changes, one feature has stayed just the same—the benign spirit that haunts the place.

Staff at the B&B speak fondly of the curiosity in their building. They call the ghost Carl because they have concluded that he is the spirit of a man who ran the hotel during one of its earlier incarnations. Carl had no heirs when he died, so all of his worldly possessions were simply left in the hotel. One of the current managers has learned to respect the fact that the kitchen she where works was once Carl's domain. For this reason, she is no longer surprised when utensils go missing. She knows they will be returned eventually.

Carl is a busy soul. He can be heard moving furniture around at all hours of the night and day. When those sounds are heard, there are usually accompanying vibrations on the floors. But when employees look into the room from which the noises have come, they never find anyone inside or anything out of place.

Phantom on Film

The Skykomish Hotel in Skykomish, just east of Seattle, has such bold spirits in residence that they have even been captured on film. As ghost hunter Tim Dennehy wandered through the corridors of the old hotel, a camera operator captured images of eerie orbs of light following Dennehy's every step.

When I phoned to ask if anything new had occurred in the ghostly realm at the hotel, a desk clerk named Laurie casually informed me that "nothing out of the ordinary" has happened with the ghost lately. "Just the usual," Laurie said. "You'll see movements in the corner of your eye and there's nothing there. Doors slam, things go missing—that sort of thing. I've been here two and a half years, so I'm used to it by now."

It sounds as though all of the hotel's "regulars"—the natural beings and the supernatural—continue to get along well!

A Singing Waiter?

Both the Grant House and the Hidden House Restaurant in historic Vancouver are home to ghosts. The ghost of a thin, melancholy-looking man, presumed to be a former military officer, resides upstairs in a front bedroom at Grant House. He has been heard walking along an empty corridor and down a set of stairs.

The ghost of Hidden House is thought to originate in considerably more recent times, and he is as lively as spirit as you're ever likely to encounter. He locks doors from the inside, calls out the employees' names, and plays with the silverware. But it's his singing that really sends shivers down people's spines.

Chapter 3

GHOSTS IN PUBLIC

I'm frequently asked to name my favorite ghost story, and I find that a very difficult request to fulfill. So many of the tales I've collected over the years have been extraordinary that it is virtually impossible to name one above the rest. One type of supernatural story does stand out for me, however— tales of ghosts in public places.

When large numbers of people with nothing in common witness identical signs of an otherworldly presence at the same place or time, those encounters are especially difficult to dismiss.

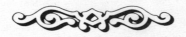

The Ghosts Underground

The first time I took the Seattle Underground Tour, I was so intrigued by the area that the desire to see it again became something of an obsession. This place, I was quite certain, was either the most cleverly mocked-up piece of property I'd ever seen or it was the most haunted spot in all of North America. Whichever the case may be, I was definitely hooked and simply had to do the tour a second time. This was no small feat—I live hundreds of miles away from Seattle. Nevertheless, I managed to plan my family's summer vacation to allow for a couple of days on the coast. While everyone else had lined up general sightseeing opportunities, all I wanted to do was explore the Underground again.

On the second visit I was, if anything, even more taken by the unique architectural venue. This time, however, I wasn't as overwhelmed by the strangeness of what I was seeing and was able to appreciate and admire additional aspects of the Seattle Underground. As a business, for example, the Underground is a study in brilliance. The owners have taken what was effectively a blemish on the history of the city and turned it into a madly popular tourist attraction. This is quite an accomplishment in itself.

While all of this was fascinating, I still didn't have the answer to my original question. Is the Seattle Underground haunted? Because I am a writer, I am fortunate enough to get away with asking outlandish questions for perfectly legitimate reasons. After investigating the history surrounding the Underground and deciding to write a minimum of two magazine articles about it, I contacted Dana Cox, resident historian of the Underground Tour.

Some of the thousands who have toured the Seattle Underground have seen ghosts and other paranormal phenomena.

Given my love of ghostlore, it's not surprising that one of the articles I proposed to write would detail the Underground's status as a haunted venue. And, of course, to write that one I needed to determine whether the eerie feelings that I had experienced in the place were naturally occurring or merely the result of some carefully constructed atmosphere.

Much to my surprise, the truth lay somewhere between my two initial premises. Although the Seattle Underground is certainly accepted by a great many people as being haunted, numerous employees, all of whom have spent many hours in the subterranean labyrinth, have never seen or even sensed anything supernatural. As for the place being purposely created to look spooky, well, the original settlers—those responsible for the development of the city of Seattle—are the ones who should take the credit (or blame) for that. Without their rather distorted principles, none of the fun, or the ghosts, of this inimitable urban environment would exist.

Seattle, as we know it today, is actually the second incarnation of the city. The first consisted of a maze of wooden sidewalks surrounding wooden buildings that, because the area was practically below sea level, had to sit atop stilts—wooden ones, of course. This thoughtless scheme for urban development was nothing more than a fire waiting to happen. On June 6, 1889, the inevitable occurred. A 24-year-old apprentice in a cabinetmaker's shop knocked over a vat of hot glue. The fire caused by the young man's clumsiness effectively reduced the entire city to cinders. Amazingly, there was no loss of life.

After the dust settled and the timbers cooled, the city fathers should have realized they now had the opportunity to rebuild properly. They could raise the level of the land so that the replacement buildings would not have to perch precariously on supports. Unfortunately, this process would have taken more time and money than the pioneer entrepreneurs were willing to spend. To ensure that the city's commerce could resume as quickly as possible, the businessmen erected replacement buildings immediately, while planning to raise the land around those structures at a later date.

This meant that shops and services were open and operating again quickly—but it also meant that what was currently a ground floor location would, once enough landfill had accumulated around it, become a basement with no direct access to the outdoors. The level that had been built as the second floor soon became street level.

For a while, particularly during the Klondike Gold Rush in the late 1890s, the subterranean stores continued to operate. Demonstrating their typical consideration, the city planners placed ladders at street corners. If people wanted to access shops that were now below ground, they simply climbed down the ladder, went into the stores to shop, and climbed back up to the street when their transactions were complete.

Not surprisingly, this system quickly lost its appeal. The underground stores attracted fewer and fewer customers. Businesses that could afford the move transferred their facilities up a story. Predictably, the quality of businesses remaining beneath street level declined steadily until, eventually, respectable people simply didn't go underground at all. At that point, Seattle's cellar became home to some fairly disreputable establishments.

In 1907, the area was condemned as being unfit for human habitation and was officially vacated. Unofficially, however, the basement maze became a shelter to vagrants—and to ghosts.

That period was, to date, the longest chapter in the history of the Seattle Underground. Little changed from 1907 until the mid-1960s, when an imaginative and energetic journalist named Bill Speidel began his work to resurrect the Underground. Speidel argued that the area was a legitimate and unique piece of local history, and that if he was interested in this aspect of Seattle's past, then maybe other folks would be, too. It took many volunteers thousands of hours to muck through the years of detritus, but Speidel's dream finally did come true. In May of 1965, on the day that the Seattle Chamber of Commerce designated as "Know Your Seattle Day," 500 curious citizens lined up for a glimpse at this strange remnant of their city's history. The interest in seeing the Underground has never waned since.

Today the tour business is owned and operated by Bill Speidel's descendants, and it continues to draw impressive crowds. No less than two dozen tour guides escort more than 200,000 curious people through the catacombs each year. While the area is undeniably fascinating, the tour guides are so much fun that they, too, must take credit for the popularity of "The Forgotten City"—the area that two of my guides, in classic deadpan, referred to as "a celebration of stupidity."

Although they're all personable and well informed, not all of the tour guides have seen, or even acknowledge, the ghosts in the Underground. Historian Dana Cox graciously put me in touch with longtime tour leader Janet Ryan, who spoke openly and at length about the ghostly manifestations that she has seen while showing visitors through the catacombs.

Janet has frequently seen the ghost of the Underground when she has been leading groups of children on the excursion. Because children are so much more open to paranormal phenomena than adults, I immediately wondered if Janet thought there was a connection between children being present and ghosts being visible. Janet kindly explained that, although my theory was solid, my reasoning wasn't. Children's attention spans and activity levels are simply different than those of adults. Kids require more stops along the route, and it has most often been during those additional stops that Janet has seen the entity.

"I have seen him twice," Janet said. "It was the same gentleman both times. He was just outside the bank vault. I don't always stop at that particular spot, so I might have just been in the right place at the right time. He didn't move or speak, but he was a solid image. There was no fog, no vapors. He didn't look like a living being. He wasn't see-through, but he wasn't three-dimensional, either. He was tall—I'd estimate 5'11" to 6'1". He had brown hair, parted on the left side. He had a large unwaxed mustache which curled up toward his cheeks."

The entity's old-fashioned clothing made Janet think that he had worked in the Underground during its heyday. "He had on a white button-up shirt with a band collar. He was casually dressed, and his sleeves were rolled up a bit. He wore brown twill pants and no tie."

Because the image neither moved nor spoke, Janet had the impression that she was witnessing an imprint on the psychic landscape rather than an actual apparition. Oddly, none of the

Tour guide Janet Ryan believes that the ghostly image she has seen is that of the former bank manager.

children seemed to see what Janet did, but she does suspect that the exuberance of the kids might have helped to attract the spirit. Not wishing to upset any of the children, she finished the tour and said nothing about seeing the ghost.

The area in which Janet saw the man's image was especially interesting because, as Dana Cox explains, it is the spot where he began telling people in the 1980s that they were about to go through a section of the Underground that he believed had been used as an auxiliary bank vault. "I identified where the vault would be by describing it verbally," Cox said. "I told them that they could also be certain that they were in the old vault because it got colder at that spot, which it does. I said that this was because the vault is haunted. Within a year, Johnny Moses, a respected local Native American shaman, asked if he could do a healing ceremony in the Underground. He believed that there had been a pre-European contact native burial ground in our neighborhood. We happily gave him permission. Where did he chose to perform his ceremony? You guessed it—the bank vault!"

Of course, Janet is not the only person to have detected phantoms in the Underground. In the spring of 1995, as she was leading a group back up to street level, Janet noticed that a trio of women who had been with her throughout the tour now seemed to be quite agitated. She approached the threesome and asked if any of them was feeling ill. She was assured that, physically, all the women felt fine. When pressed, one of the three replied rather cryptically, "There were a lot of visitors by the bank vault." Janet soon realized that they had spotted the ghost and confessed that she had, on other occasions, also seen the entity. Janet's unquestioning acceptance of their statement gave the women the courage to elaborate and reveal that they had also seen three Native American people. Those sightings didn't surprise Janet, as she had been led to understand that a Native burial ground had existed in the spot long before Europeans began immigrating to the area.

As for the specter by the bank, Janet still wonders if he could be a former bank manager. "I've always figured he was still on the job. He's checking on his gold. He may not even be aware that the gold isn't there any more. I think he's just really dedicated."

And so is Janet. She's been a guide at the Underground since 1992. During the intervening years, "maybe three dozen people have asked me about ghosts or spirits in the Underground. I don't know how many of those asking had seen or felt something. You wouldn't generally expect someone in a group of people to ask that question without a reason. Some people will occasionally hang back and ask me if I've ever seen anything in the Underground. When they get a positive reaction, they seem to think that it's cool. One of the women said, 'The walls absolutely shimmered with spirits.'"

Janet's stories helped me to accept and understand my own fascination with the haunted Underground. After learning that an episode of the 1970s television series *The Night Stalker*, starring Darren McGavin, had revolved around the Underground, I knew that I was definitely not the only person who had found the area innately eerie and intriguing.

The Spirit at the Station

Many theories have attempted to explain the existence of ghosts. One school of thought maintains that what we identify as a ghost is merely leftover energy. This theory is useful in explaining why places where traumas have occurred tend to be haunted. It also could explain why poltergeists are especially attracted to adolescents, whose developing bodies are highly energized by surging hormones. At a more mundane level, we often see that spirits are intrigued by electrical energy and can draw attention to themselves by turning appliances, such as washing machines, televisions and VCRs, on and off. Imagine, then, what fun a ghost would have when surrounded by the electrical devices and energy at a radio station.

KNDX-FM in Yakima is no longer on the air, but during the 1960s it was a going concern—and a very haunted one. Perhaps the most intriguing facet of this ghost story is that individually, without consulting one another, all of the employees began to refer to the spirit at the station as "Fred."

It is not known whether Fred had always resided in the small brick building that housed the station or if he was attracted to the energy created by all of the broadcast equipment. What is known for certain is that even when they knew they were in the building alone, employees always had the sense of an additional presence.

Kirk Williamson, who worked at KNDX, felt that he was rarely alone in the station's control room. Rather than being frightened by the constant presence, though, Kirk was reassured by it and would actually feel uneasy if he didn't sense that Fred was with him.

Unlike other radio station ghosts I've heard about, Fred did not play practical jokes. He was content to merely be present.

Eternally Dancing

In 1933, on West Beach—south and west of Pier 70—dozens of witnesses watched in fascination as the apparition of an elderly Native American man suddenly materialized. The manifestation seemed to be unaware of those around him. The dignified vision walked along the sand of the beach slowly, but with seeming purpose. After traveling several hundred yards, the man's image simply vanished into thin air.

Unfortunately, no reports remain to indicate whether any of the witnesses to the ghostly appearance and disappearance thought to check for footprints in the sand.

That sighting was vaguely reminiscent of one that was frequently reported at the Glenacres Golf Course in Seattle. The image of a naked man was frequently seen on the trail to the course during a 20-year period from 1940 to 1960. The vision, said to be performing a Native dance, eluded all attempts by citizens and police to catch it. Many believe that the golf course was built on an ancient Native burial ground, but archival searches haven't supported that theory. The reason for the haunting remains as elusive as the ghost itself.

Ghost Lights?

The public has long been curious about the mysterious lights that are frequently spotted near Mount Rainier, south and east of Seattle. Although many have speculated that these lights are emanating from UFOs, it seems equally likely that they are actually examples of ghost lights, or ignes fatui. The lights that are reportedly seen in that area usually meet the description of just such a supernatural phenomena. The orbs range from roughly the size of a softball to being as large as a beach ball. They are described as varying from a bright white—so intense that it is almost blue—to a pale yellow or dull shade of red.

Ghost lights are among the oldest reported forms of haunting. They are most frequently seen in or near cemeteries, mountains, roads, lakes or railroad tracks. We can safely assume, therefore, that the mysterious lights so often seen around Mount Rainier are not signs of life from another planet but examples of "afterlife" from another realm of our own planet.

Haunted Hall

Some amazingly loyal citizens have called Tacoma home. This group includes the phantom responsible for ringing the bells in the tower of Old City Hall at midnight, even after the mechanism necessary to make the bells ring had long been disengaged. Suspecting that intruders were breaking in and playing the bells as a practical joke, manager Jim Brewster spent a night in the building. By the next morning he was convinced that the hall was secure but haunted.

"There is a spirit up here," Brewster stated emphatically.

Security guards who work in the building agree. They have been led on wild ghost chases throughout the halls by "fleeting shadows"—never finding anything that could logically have caused such shapes to appear.

Authorities have also received inexplicable false alarms from within the building. People walking past the haunted hall at night report watching lights turning on and off. When these sightings are reported, they are investigated thoroughly. Time after time, the findings are the same—the room from which the lights were shining is found to be completely dark and empty.

Mummy was There

Like many museums, Tacoma's Washington State Historical Society Museum was, at one time, haunted. One of the ghosts was positively identified as President Abraham Lincoln's widow, Mary. Appropriately, her ghost was seen near the display of artifacts associated with the slain leader. It was also there that a guard stood and stared in astonishment as a chair glided effortlessly—and apparently magically—across a marble floor. However, the dignified phantom of Mrs. Lincoln hasn't been seen since renovations to enlarge the museum were begun in 1973.

Although the staff no doubt missed Mary Todd Lincoln's presence, they were certainly not left alone. The remaining ghost was quite intrigued by the elevator. He or she would cause the empty elevator, in the equally empty building, to propel itself from floor to floor.

During a period when the museum was hosting the display of an Egyptian mummy, spirits associated with the exhibit were generally blamed for malfunctions in the building's electrical system. Lights that were turned on would not stay lit and alarm bells would ring for no logical reason. The museum's security guards frequently noted isolated cold spots where there should not have been any drafts.

Much has changed now. The displays have been rotated, and even the location of the museum has been moved. The old ghosts are no longer reported—but that doesn't necessarily mean that the new building is free of phantoms.

Haunted Courthouse

In April of 1959, the *Tacoma News Tribune* ran an article indicating that, by that time, two ghosts had been in residence at the old Pierce County Courthouse for "half a century." Anyone who was familiar with the history of the building could not have been particularly astonished to learn that the place was haunted. After all, archival documents refer to numerous hangings that were performed in—or from the window of—the courthouse's "dusty, dingy attic" during the early years of the 20th century.

Many folks believed that the resident spirits were those of E.L. Boyce and Albert Michaud. Legal records show that each of the two men was found guilty of killing his own wife. That their spirits stayed behind to haunt the building is hardly surprising. What does seem a bit odd, however, are the descriptions of the enitities' spectral antics. Presumably both Boyce and Michaud were, at the time of their executions, angry and menacing individuals—but in death their presences were described, almost fondly, as being "mischievous."

Because the stately old courthouse no longer serves any judicial function—and because the new county buildings are touted as having "bright, ghost-proof lights"—chances are good that both Boyce and Michaud have finally left the Pierce County legal system in peace.

Spooky Shadle

By purest definition, this account may not be a ghost story. If a ghost is the energy left over from a human life, then at least one of the people who witnessed these chilling events didn't feel that they had been in the presence of a ghost. It is equally possible, however, that what we have here is a ghost story. There is, after all, much about the spirit world that we do not understand. Either way, the tale is, without a doubt, scary—and it clearly recounts a brush with the paranormal.

The gentleman in this story, whom we'll call Tim, began his recollection of the unnerving experience by stressing how entirely safe he considers the city of Spokane to be. It is a city he knows well and one in which he does not typically feel threatened. Tim even added that Shadle, the district in which he and his former girlfriend shared this experience, is an exceptionally quiet area.

And so it was that Tim and Des, his girlfriend at the time, were enjoying a pleasant late-evening stroll to a coffee shop on a summer night in 1995. It was past midnight, but they knew that the place would still be open. As they made their way toward the restaurant, the couple probably paid no attention to the shadows created by street lamps along their route. Then the light they were walking directly beneath—the one at the southeast corner of Cedar Street and Garland Avenue—suddenly went out.

Given that both Tim and Des are pragmatic folks, neither of them prone to paranoia or flights of fancy, the coincidence of the light burning out or mysteriously turning off did not strike them as being anything to fear. But what happened almost immediately thereafter did scare them rather badly.

"We'd gone about another four feet, when we were struck by a large pocket of cold air," Tim recalled. He remembered that this "pocket" was not stationary but "moved with enough force to almost knock us off balance. It shot between us, and stopped abruptly behind us. It seemed to stay there, and spread out—like it was wrapping itself around us."

In unspoken agreement, the couple ran from the spot and did not look back until they had reached the opposite end of the block. Only then did they risk taking a glance behind them.

"We looked back, and saw a pale grey cloud sitting there. The thing looked to be about five feet wide, and eight to nine feet in height. It was hard to tell, exactly, from that distance," Tim recalled.

While admitting that he had no known psychic abilities, Tim did acknowledge that the menacing current of air that formed this pale grey cloud left him with "three distinct impressions."

"First, I felt that it wasn't anything human—and that it never had been. Secondly, I believed that it was very hostile. Lastly, I felt that it was intelligent ... it was not mindless."

To this day, Tim has no real idea of what to call the force that interfered with the couple's trip to the coffee shop. He just knows that it frightened him more than "anything in my life."

Nevertheless, Tim and Des took exactly the same route just a few nights later. But this time when the same street lamp went out as they walked under it, they didn't stick around to see what might happen next. They turned tail and ran for safety. Ever since, both together and separately, Tim and Des have been careful to take a detour en route to their favorite coffee shop.

Unofficial Ghosts

While researching ghost stories, I frequently encounter some interesting contradictions. Representatives from public buildings often adopt a firm policy of denying any knowledge of ghosts in or around their property—even though many of the properties are widely known to be haunted places. This zipped-lip policy can lead to awkward situations, especially for staff members who have witnessed ghostly manifestations. A world-famous luxury hotel in the Rocky Mountains is an excellent example. Management there vehemently denies the existence of ghosts in their hostelry. When I mentioned this to a long-time employee, he merely chuckled and asked, "Do you know what they're going to do with the ghosts then?"

In other haunted spots, some of the staff will speak candidly—but only on a one-to-one, off-the-record basis. This seems to have been the situation at the Fort Wright Historical Museum. The official stance was that the building was not haunted. However, curious ghost lovers ferreted out some pretty amazing tales about the old place. Even a cursory look at the history of this building, which is one of the oldest at Fort Wright College and had a varied history prior to its use as a museum, reveals ideal conditions for the existence of a spirit or two.

According to the reports I have studied, the resident ghosts may have been the spirits of souls who did not realize that they were dead. Most of the activity in and around the building consisted of disturbances made by phantoms who seemed to be going about their everyday lives—in another dimension. Doors and windows opened and closed, apparently on their own. Disembodied footsteps echoed throughout corridors, and lights that were turned off would come on when no one was near the switch. After a time, those same lights would, just as mysteriously, be turned off again.

At least one of the spirits in the museum had an emotional reaction to music. A student worker was singing while she went about her shift. Just a few bars into her tune, doors in the otherwise empty building began slamming closed. It's probably safe to guess that the young woman did not go on to a career as a singer! Despite such a negative reaction to the human voice, several people have heard ghostly singing coming from the building after it has been vacated and secured for the night.

Another ghost—the one on the third floor—is thought to be a woman. She may have been associated in life with one or more of the dolls displayed there. Of course, no one can be sure.

Although not officially recognized, there have been many reports of spectral activity in this historical building at Fort Wright College.

The Mayor is Still Hanging Around

Many people have reported seeing the figure of a well-dressed man walking onto the Interstate Bridge in downtown Vancouver. He appears in a solid form but then vanishes instantly. Researchers believe the ghost is the spirit of Grover R. Percival, a former mayor of Vancouver.

The last time the man was seen alive, he was walking onto that same bridge. Many of those who were Vancouverites at the time clearly recall greeting Percival as he walked past on that dark October evening. Nothing in his demeanor suggested that he was about to take his own life—but that is exactly what he was planning to do. His body was found the next day; the former mayor had hanged himself. To this day, no one knows why Percival would have taken such drastic action. They only know that he is apparently doomed in death to retrace, over and over again, the final few steps of his life.

Military Manifestations

If the population statistics in historic Fort Vancouver, Washington, included both corporeal and ethereal beings, the total numbers recorded might well double. There are so many ghosts in the town that organized ghost-walk tours are offered.

Most of the hauntings center around former military installations. The buildings that once were Officers' Row are absolutely teeming with spirits. A fun-loving father and daughter duo from long ago still flit in and out of view. They are, apparently, just continuing on with the happy relationship they enjoyed during their lifetimes.

The ghost of Ellen Waite, however, is not so happy. She, too, was the daughter of a military man, but her life was cut short by a drowning accident. Ellen's melancholy spirit has spent the years since searching for Joseph, the man she loved. Her premature death robbed the couple of their planned life together, so she searches in vain, hoping to instead share her afterlife with him.

Spirits have also manifested in other spooky ways. Telephones in buildings along the row have been known to ring. That would hardly be unusual, except that all of the phones were unplugged and removed at the time the officers' quarters were abandoned. In another instance, the freshly brewed contents of a coffee pot inexplicably disappeared. Perhaps the strangest ghostly prank of all came when the tiny speaker on a company's fax machine suddenly began broadcasting a program from a radio station specializing in religious shows.

It would be a surprise if the barracks at Fort Vancouver were not haunted. In 1982, workers trying to unearth a water pipe under the facility's auditorium got the shock of their lives when they unexpectedly began digging up human remains. It seems that, approximately 100 years earlier, workers responsible for moving existing graves from that area failed to pay appropriate attention to detail—they moved the coffins found under head-stones, but if there were no markers the workmen apparently left the graves as they were and allowed construction to proceed on top of them.

The result was a very haunted building. Footfalls were heard echoing in deserted stairwells and resounding through empty cor-ridors. Doors slammed closed when no one was near them and workers heard voices from vacant areas.

In 1993, the final resting place of these long-dead commoners had to be disturbed again. This time, Roy Wilson, a Native American holy man, was called in to perform a ceremony to free the spirits from their earthly realm. The ritual may have come too late, though, because people still report hearing phantom foot-steps when this and other buildings in the area are unpopulated.

The ghosts in the old Barracks Hospital (Building 614) have been forced to put up with many changes to their ghostly abode. Throughout the renovations and additions, these spirits have seemed determined to continue holding court. One particular phantom is evidently intrigued by modern-day office equipment. He is frequently heard—but never seen—operating the photo-copier on the first floor.

Doors to the offices on upper floors are virtually impossible to keep locked; employees who securely lock the doors at night find them unlocked in the morning. Even so, no one has ever found any evidence of intruders or a break-in. A similar phenomenon has occurred with the electric lights in the area. Lighting fixtures which had been turned off at night were found burning brightly the following morning.

Phantom Footsteps

For years, special dances hosted by the staff and students of Yakima High School were held in the National Guard Armory, located at South 3rd Street and East Walnut Avenue. These popular events were well attended—by the living and by a gaggle of ghosts.

The Armory was erected at the beginning of World War I. It served as a drill hall, mess hall and firing range, and the facility was made available for community use as often as possible. So, in addition to the school's formal dances, the Armory was frequently used as a venue for concerts. Some of the biggest names in the entertainment industry—such as rock and roll legends Ike and Tina Turner, Little Richard and Fats Domino—performed in the cavernous old brick building.

While these musical giants played, it is likely that at least some of their audience was invisible. Even the stalwart members of the armed services who occupied the structure during the week reported hearing phantom sounds. The Drill Hall was a focal point for this haunting. Office workers who thought they were the only people in the building would hear the door to the Drill Hall open. Sometimes it would close again almost immediately, but other times the living occupants of the building would be treated to the sounds of several dozen sets of footsteps marching, in unison, into the room. Then, in an equally synchronized manner, the footsteps would cease. Each time this happened, the workers would immediately hurry to the hall to investigate. No one was ever there—no one who could be seen, that is.

Occasionally, a loud male voice could be heard barking out what sounded like a command or a terse question. When this happened, the first voice would always be followed by quieter ones, presumably enlisted men responding to the order or inquiry. If anyone ever saw the spirits haunting the Armory, those sightings were not reported.

The Drill Hall is gone now, torn down in 1994 to make room for a building that houses a police station. Wouldn't it would be interesting to learn if any extra officers are ever heard to answer at roll call?

Wardrobe Wraith

A children's clothing store in the south-central city of Kennewick hosts a most charming entity. The owners and staff of the store feel such fondness for the ghost that they have even given him a name. They call their resident revenant "Freddy," even though a growing collection of evidence seems to indicate that he actually had another identity in life.

The shop's owner was most acutely aware that not all of the occupants of the store were operating on the same plane of existence when she first opened the doors in the morning. Large, heavy racks of merchandise that she had left in one location when locking up the night before would be found in completely different spots. Lights that had been conscientiously turned off at closing were burning away in the morning. Each time, the owners were certain that no one had been in the store during the intervening hours.

Over the course of time the employees began to sense that the haunting was somehow centered around the basement boiler room. This premise fits with one theory about who the ghost might be. At least one version of local history states that, years ago, part of the building had been used as a gambling den. To keep the participants safe from the long arm of the law, gamblers were required to make their way—by means of a hidden staircase—to a secret room near the area that now houses the furnace. The ghost may be the fragment of a gambler's soul, perhaps hoping to win back some of his losses.

Another theory frequently ventured to explain the ghost's existence is just as convincing. George Sherk, Kennewick's mayor from 1913 to 1924, ran a retail establishment in the building now occupied by the clothing store. The man died prematurely in an automobile accident, so it is quite possible that his restless spirit is the apparition seen roaming about the place.

No matter what his identity in life, staff members continue to refer to the spirit by the nickname "Freddy" and the ghost continues to enjoy puzzling the staff with his antics. These hijinks include balancing a small, unused safe at a precarious angle on an old bed left behind in the boiler room. The building's current owner has admitted to being startled when the boiler itself seemingly reacts noisily to any person entering that room. But overall she feels that the presence in her store is at worst a nuisance and at best an extra degree of security.

Chapter 4

STAGE FRIGHT

Actors, and the crews that support their theatrical efforts, tend to be a devoted, dedicated and emotional group of individuals. (They're also highly superstitious, but that's another, equally interesting, story.)

The actor's job is an odd one: In a highly contrived setting, with the help of the others, he or she works to convince another group of individuals—the audience— that something fictional is actually fact. Judging by the number of haunted theaters, this kind of highly charged atmosphere is a successful breeding ground for phantoms.

Phantom Feminists?

At the Harvard Exit Theater in Seattle, patrons are not so much movie house customers as they are guests in an unusual and luxurious home. Tucked away on East Roy Street in the Capitol Hill region, the stately appearance of the three-story, red brick 1920s-era building belies its purpose. Of course, that the structure began life as the headquarters for the Women's Century Club explains much of this incongruity. It also serves as an explanation for why the theater is so very haunted.

Members of the Women's Century Club were some of Seattle's earliest feminists. These were strong personalities who believed in and worked toward the then-radical goal of equality for women. Given this intensity of emotion and purpose, it is no wonder that a few of the suffragettes' spirits have stayed on long after their deaths.

Janet Wainwright, who managed the theater for nearly 10 years, declared simply that there were "always paranormal happenings" in the building. After a while, she learned to take the encounters in stride, but the first instance gave her quite a start. As manager, she was required to be at the theater before any of the other staff members arrived. On this particular day, Janet unlocked the well-secured doors and made her way to the glorious main lobby, which retains a 1920s atmosphere and is adorned with a grand piano and chandelier. The area is furnished with comfortable chairs for the patrons to enjoy while they wait to enter the auditorium. Much to Janet's surprise, a woman with her hair piled up on her head in a bun and wearing a long floral dress was sitting and reading in one of those chairs.

Shocked that someone had been able to get in before she'd unlocked the building, the manager steeled her nerve to confront the intruder. Just as she composed herself, Janet realized that the woman at whom she was staring was just slightly see-through. Seconds later, as Janet continued to stare in fascination and horror, the woman slowly vanished. In retrospect, that one incident set the stage, so to speak, for the many encounters yet to transpire.

Alice McCullough, who worked at the theater in a number of capacities, remembers being told that, on a few occasions, the same apparition of a reading woman would calmly look up from her book and smile in acknowledgment of whichever human being had just come into the theater. Then the ghost would turn off the lamp beside her and walk out of the room.

Those comfortable chairs in the lobby are grouped around a large fireplace. Tradition dictates that a fire is always burning in the hearth for moviegoers to enjoy as they wait to watch the show. Lighting the fire was always one of the first jobs Janet accomplished when she got to work. Every now and then, however, she was greeted by the pleasant sight of a fire already burning brightly in the hearth. On those days, she would also find that the chairs in the lobby had been rearranged as if people who were no longer there—or were no longer visible—had been enjoying a chat around the fireplace. Photographers have also taken snapshots of what they thought was a vacant lobby, only to develop their film and find images of people sitting on chairs that had appeared to be unoccupied.

On other days, of course, Janet would have to build and light the fire herself. On some of those occasions she did not have to walk into a darkened lobby—because she would see the spirit of a tall woman leaving the room and flipping the light switches as she went.

Janet Wainwright is certainly not the only person to be aware of the ghosts at the Harvard Exit Theater. An employee who was doing paperwork in the second floor administration area was startled to hear a woman sobbing. Following the sound, he found the person he had overheard—a woman who was crying piteously.

As he approached her to offer whatever comfort he could, the manifestation vaporized before his eyes. This encounter was bizarre enough in its own right, but it was made even more strange by the fact that the hauntings have usually been restricted to the main lobby and to the third floor.

Alan Blangy, who managed the theater after Janet Wainwright's tenure, was a skeptic when he began working there. Even so, he did admit to some puzzling feelings of discomfort—almost an irrational sense that something in the building was hostile toward him. One night that "sense" transformed into a specific antagonist. As he and his assistant manager were leaving and locking the building for the night, Blangy heard a loud noise from inside the theater. He quickly unlocked the door and ran back in. No one should have been inside, but as Blangy walked into the auditorium he clearly saw the door to the fire escape closing. The concerned manager ran toward the door, arriving just before it was fully closed. He grabbed the handle and tried to jerk the door open. Much to his surprise, those efforts were met with considerable resistance. It felt as though someone was standing on the other side of the door, tugging at it, trying to counter Blangy's leverage. For several moments the theater manager and his unseen combatant each pulled on the door, until finally, with a concerted effort, Blangy was able to close the door.

The assistant manager heard the scuffle and ran back into the building to see what was happening. He reached Blangy's side just as the manager finally overpowered his invisible opponent. The two immediately opened the door wide and hurried through it, hoping to catch the intruder. Much to their surprise, they found themselves staring out at an empty fire escape staircase—30 feet above the ground. Because less than five seconds had elapsed, whomever or whatever had been pulling against the door would certainly not have had time to make a getaway down the stairs. Stranger still, these rickety metal stairs were virtually impossible to walk on without making a terrible racket—yet neither Alan Blangy nor his assistant had heard any sound at all.

Eventually the two were satisfied that the building was secure. For the second time that night, they locked up and left the theater. Oddly, from that moment on, Blangy never again felt uncomfortable in the building—quite to the contrary, he now felt welcomed each time he came to work.

It was a projectionist who had one of the most frightening experiences. He arrived at work and was startled to find the movie already playing. He hurried to the projection booth and grabbed at the door handle, hoping to catch the prankster in the act. Unfortunately, he didn't succeed—because the door was locked from the inside. The projectionist unlocked the door with his key and found the booth empty. Whatever entity had started the movie prematurely is also credited with performing the annoying trick of moving canisters of film around the booth.

One of the most common ghost sightings in the Harvard Exit takes place on the third floor. People frequently report seeing the apparition of a woman. When they turn to get a better look, the image simply disappears. One of those revenants may be Bertha Landes, who was not only a member of the Century Club but also Seattle's first woman mayor. When a museum in Seattle's beautiful Smith Tower assembled a display in honor of Landes and her contributions to the city, it was generally accepted that her spirit was to blame for some otherwise inexplicable occurrences—such as supplies being mysteriously moved about at the exhibition. Some people even maintained that they had seen Bertha Landes's image floating near the artifacts on display.

One more curious note about the female ghosts in this haunting: The Century Club is still an organization whose members meet in the building on East Roy Street where it all began. None of the members, however, will discuss or even entertain the possibility that their predecessors have left the old clubhouse haunted.

Although most of the ghosts at the Harvard Exit Theater are women, there have been sightings of male image. He is slightly translucent, portly and dressed in old-fashioned attire. This presence may date back to a time before the current building was constructed. Records show that there was a murder in the house that previously stood at that address.

The Harvard Exit Theater is more like a regular house than your typical movie house—and this house is definitely haunted.

Ghost on Guard

The management team at the Moore Theatre in downtown Seattle believe that they, too, have a ghost. Built in 1907, the Moore is the city's oldest surviving theater. The magnificent showplace was bankrolled by James A. Moore, the flashy builder behind much of the early development of downtown Seattle and Capitol Hill. The theater has a simple exterior with Italian and Byzantine terracotta details, but its lavish interior is Gothic in style with mosaic floors and a lobby adorned in solid onyx and marble, carved wood, stained glass, and a ceiling fresco in rose, cream and gold.

For its first two decades, the Moore was the Seattle venue for the world-famous Orpheum vaudeville circuit. When the Orpheum organization built its own theater nearby in 1927, the Moore's vaudeville days were over. During the 1930s, Cecilia Schultz, one of the founders of the arts scene in Seattle, took over the leadership of the Moore and presented many of the best European and American singers, musicians, theatrical troupes and dancers of the time—first-class performers such as Sarah Bernhardt, Lily Langtry, the Barrymores, Marie Dressler, and Anna Pavlova.

In 1974 the Moore was awarded landmark status and placed on the National Register of Historic Places, but the theater had fallen on hard times financially. Between 1975 and 1980 it was operated as a movie house called the "Moore-Egyptian." The Moore returned to stage arts when the film impresarios lost the lease and moved the Egyptian Theatre to a different building a few blocks away. After extensive renovations and restorations, the Moore has been returned to its former glory and equipped with new and larger seats. The grand old theater is one again a popular venue for dramatic arts, concerts, lectures, and other public events.

The protective spirit of the Moore seems to heartily endorse the improvements made to the former vaudeville house. Although the shock of realizing they were in the presence of a phantom has frightened some members of the theater's staff, the ghost has never done anything that could be construed as malicious in any way. The ghost has never been seen, but it has been felt in the form of a foul odor and a sudden, unexplainable blast of cold air.

Ghost Cracks Them Up

Another haunted Seattle theater is the local landmark known as the Neptune, located in the "U. District" near the University of Washington—and the ghosts there have actually been seen. A janitor reported watching the manifestation of a woman wearing a long, dark-colored gown make its way across his line of vision. He knew for sure that he was not seeing a human being because the image did not walk on the floor but floated approximately five inches above it.

This may have been the same entity that Pam Sprowl saw while she was manager of the Neptune Theater. Pam described what she had seen as "a lady with dark hair" although "definitely not human." This time, however, the figure appeared to be dressed in white. Other workers have identified a presence that they call "the gray lady." She may have been the ghost who was indirectly responsible for breaking the top of the candy counter.

The incident occurred one night after a late showing of *The Rocky Horror Picture Show.* Nighttime cleaners were taking a break. As they stood in the lobby sipping soft drinks, one of them caught sight of a girl in a gray dress. He called out to her to explain that the theater was closed and that she shouldn't still be there. The words were no sooner out of his mouth than the man realized that he could see right through the woman. A few seconds later, the apparition vanished. The poor worker was so terrified that he dropped the can of soda he had been holding and, in doing so, cracked the glass shelf that formed the top of the candy counter.

Theater painter Jeff Kurtti is very accepting of the ghosts at the Neptune, but he did readily admit to being somewhat unnerved by the distinct feeling of someone—an invisible someone—rushing past him.

Mason's Manifestation

The enormous Temple Theater on Saint Helens Avenue in Tacoma has long been accepted as being home to a ghost. The building is a former Masonic Lodge, so it is not surprising that people have only seen the apparitions of men here. One specter, wearing a long robe, frequently stands at an upstairs window, looking out to the street below. He's been heard walking in an otherwise empty building and he is also frequently seen near the building's front doors. The staff is all very aware of the haunting and refer to the ghost or ghosts simply as "Charlie."

Judy, Judy, Judy

In the Roaring Twenties, when the grand plans to build the Mount Baker Theatre in Bellingham began to unfold, it must have seemed that the reign of vaudeville would go on forever. Despite this confidence in the then-current vogue, Mount Baker Theatre architect R.C. Reamer had the foresight to include a project booth. His advance planning was soon rewarded. Just months after the theater's official opening, management enticed audiences with a real novelty—a film called *The Jazz Singer*, the world's first talking motion picture! People were fascinated. The decline of both vaudeville and silent movies had begun. Less than two years later, the stock market crashed and the Great Depression struck the final death blow to the art of vaudeville. The bright lights of opulent and extravagant vaudeville houses all over North America darkened forever.

The history of the Mount Baker Theatre has always included Judy, its resident ghost.

Fortunately for theatergoers—and for ghosts—some of those grand old halls, the Mount Baker among them, have survived and been restored. This must be especially gratifying for Judy, the ghost haunting the Mount Baker, whose presence actually predates the existence of the theater. It is believed that Judy lived and died in the house that once stood on the site. She was apparently killed in a fire that destroyed her family's home, and her spirit has been haunting the theater from its very first day.

Former house manager Margaret Mackay had a first-hand experience with Judy that she'll never forget. Current house manager Anna Marie said Margaret often described a walk through the upstairs of the lobby during which an incredibly cold blast of air seemed to move right through her. Margaret stopped walking for a minute and the lights flickered at the same time."

Former house manager Margaret Mackay felt a blast of cold air move through her in this upstairs hallway.

Perhaps that was Judy's way of wishing the house manager a good night. On another occasion, Margaret was actually able to photograph Judy's presence. Members of the camera crew from a local television show were not so fortunate while they were filming in the theater. They did, however, record the explorations of the psychically sensitive woman whom they had brought with them.

Judy has plenty of company—a psychic once sensed an entire troupe of ghosts on this stage.

"She said that there was indeed a troupe of ghosts in the theater," Anna Marie explained. "They are down on the main stage, stage left, front, downstage. They're just kind of hanging out with us."

This finding was not much of a surprise, as others had sensed much more than just Judy's presence in the grand old hall.

Still, Judy continues to be the most noticeable phantom. Judging from some of her other actions, it's probably fair to guess that Judy was a high-spirited young woman. She particularly delights in making herself known to male projectionists and stage hands.

Judy cannot be lonely in her theatrical hereafter because the psychic who visited the Mount Baker found an entire troupe of ghosts on the stage. The staff at the theater not only accept their ghostly inhabitants, but they actually speak of the spooks with evident affection. It seems that the Mount Baker Theatre and its entities are happily and inextricably entwined with one another forever.

Well-loved Shorty

If ghosts appreciate warm acceptance as much as their flesh-and-blood counterparts do, then "Shorty," the ghost at the Capitol Theatre in Yakima, must be a very contented phantom. Bonnie Hughes, the theater's Community Relations Director, indicated that she was anxious for Shorty's story to be included in this book so that he "would get the recognition he deserves." Then, to prove her point, both Bonnie and Stage Manager Roger Smith (no relation to me) went out of their way to supply me with details of the haunting in their beautiful old theater.

In some ways the building is an amazing study in contrasts. Smith describes it as "state-of-the-art sound and lighting equipment implanted in a building exhibiting [an early] 20th-century motif and décor. Computers function in a facility occupied by red velvet seats [that are] 50 years old."

The one feature that has not changed, however, is the Capitol's status as a haunted house.

"The name of the ghost is 'Shorty.' Simply 'Shorty.' No first or last name," Smith said. "No one can offer a description of Shorty. Nobody can relate a biography. His activities are manifested mostly when the theater is empty and at rest, between shows. Shorty exists just as surely as the walls of the theater stand to house his unpredictable presence."

Smith went on to detail one particularly dramatic encounter with their resident presence. "It was 1980 and the Cold War was still raging. A touring dance troupe from then-Czechoslovakia came to the Capitol Theatre for an evening performance. Security was tight because dancers were tempted to defect and seek a better life in North America."

He went on, "A performance is heavily dependent on lighting for its aesthetic and dramatic effect. Lighting changes are affected by a 'cue sheet.' This sheet is often several pages in length, detailing several hundred light changes during a presentation. One of the dances of the Czech group included a choreographed dagger fight between two rival peasants. Before the scene, much to the frustration and panic of the two dancers, one of the steel daggers [was] missing from the prop table on stage right. In a baffling coincidence, page 13 of the lighting cue sheet was [also] missing, ripped from its place in the cue sheet notebook."

Smith explained, "The lighting engineer and dancers carried on in an improvised fashion. It was only the experience and cleverness of the dancers and the lighting engineer that allowed the scene to succeed with very little sacrifice of artistic quality."

He continued, "During the dance numbers on the stage, the dressing room area was locked, owing to the possibility that dancers would defect. Also, personal valuables and expensive costumes were kept in the dressing room complex. After the final scene, the 30 dancers trooped into the dressing room area to shed their outfits. As they approached dressing room number eight, the dancers were stunned by what they saw. The missing dagger was embedded in the door to the dressing room, and page 13 of the lighting cue sheet was impaled on the point of the knife."

Smith acknowledged that "for months afterward, conjecture abounded as to the significance of the event. There was never any question that it was the work of Shorty. Whether or not the presence of a foreign dance troupe or the lamentable existence of the Cold War prompted the action of Shorty is not known."

A few years after that dramatic occurrence, Shorty was once again at work with the theater's lights. Roger Smith recalled the incident.

"In 1985, a solo opera singer was scheduled to appear at the Capitol Theatre," Smith said. "Her performance was a medley of popular opera arias. The only other person on stage with the star was the musician accompanying her on the piano. The stage lights above bathed the singer in a soft blue wash. In addition to overhead stage lights, theaters traditionally use powerful spotlights to accent the performer. Spotlights form a brightly defined circle that follows the performer across the stage."

He continued, "The opera singer gave a sterling performance and was awarded a standing ovation. When the curtain came down, the singer was quick to thank the stagehands for their diligence and competency. She especially singled out the work of the

A ghost named Shorty is a cherished member of the production team at the Capitol Theatre in Yakima.

spotlight operators, praising their smoothness and on-target work as the best she had ever experienced. The stage manager was speechless. In a perplexed voice, he told the opera singer that the two spotlight operators had both called in sick with food poisoning. There had been nobody in the spot booth operating the lights during the show."

Shorty is also generally credited with turning the stage lights on when employees were close enough to the lighting console to see that no one had touched it. But when Shorty made spotlights dance about the stage in a ballet-like sequence, Roger Smith decided it was time for action. As quickly and quietly as he could, the stage manager made his way up the stairs to the catwalks where the lights were hung. When he found footprints but nothing else, he knew that the light-dance hadn't been the work of a practical joker at all. It was simply another demonstration of Shorty's illusions. Those incidents certainly support the theory that, in life, Shorty had been involved with technical aspects of the theater.

The entity can also be a bit mischievous. He's credited with opening the grand stage curtain and with undoing some other employees' work. Roger Smith related one example. "At the conclusion of a show, ushers routinely put all of the 1500 seats in the upright position. It has been reported at least twice that the janitor has entered the theater a few hours later and found all 1500 seats in the down position."

And the specter has firmly demonstrated that he has no fondness for the sounds of rock and roll. When the Capitol Theatre hosts such shows, they experience an unusual number of technical malfunctions and the staff must work extra hard to ensure a successful show.

For the most part, though, Shorty's actions are either harmless or helpful—and he's actually been credited with saving a life. When a piece of equipment above the stage broke away and began to fall, it was on a direct path to a woman standing on stage. The object was heavy and, had it landed where it was headed, the woman would almost certainly have been killed. As another employee at the theater watched, the projectile impossibly changed course in mid-fall, likely averting a tragedy.

Over the years, changes to the structure of theater have resulted in, among other odd features, the existence of a completely inaccessible door. It is located 12 feet above the backstage area and is never used. No one even knows whether it leads to a room or simply to a blank wall. The staff calls it "Shorty's door" because, even though no one (living) ever goes near, the door is occasionally seen to be standing open. Psychics investigating the theater found a phantom heat source near the door—12 feet above the floor.

Shorty is known to have something of an unhealthy appetite. When staff leave a plate of cookies out overnight, the plate is always empty in the morning.

Management at the Capitol Theatre has no interest in trying to operate without their invisible helper. When a pair of "ghost hunters" asked to tour the haunted old theater, management agreed only if they promised not to exorcise Shorty.

Despite the staff's fondness for Shorty, very few people are comfortable with being alone in the enormous old building.

"Lone staff members have reported that late night shifts in the massive theater have witnessed unexplained noises—footsteps in deserted hallways, clanging in the ventilation shafts, the elevator running and no one on board," Roger informed me. "No staff member opts to be in the Capitol Theatre alone after midnight." Although the fears may not be justified, Roger believes that adherence to the old adage "better safe than sorry" keeps everyone happy.

By now, Shorty and the Capitol Theatre are inseparable. As Roger Smith concluded, "The Capitol Theatre is a unique building. It is special in that it is on the National Register of Historic Buildings. It is also extraordinary in that it possesses an invisible caretaker. An invisible entity. A ghost." A ghost simply named "Shorty."

Curious George

When he was asked about the Civic Theatre in Spokane being haunted, Jack Phillips, the Artistic Director replied, "I don't know that we're haunted, but we certainly do have a friend around. We have George with us here."

Phillips explained, "George does seem to like to play tricks with the electronic light board. I have been walking through the theater late at night several times when two spotlights came on, just saying 'hello.' I have to tell you that there's no malevolent sense whatsoever. Usually what happens is that one or two spotlights will simply come on, even when the [lighting] board is off. They'll come on and stay on for a while, and then they'll just go off again." But he also says that George has pulled the staff through a show under impossible circumstances. "We have had one show where there was an electrical power failure but our board worked."

This theater ghost is a slightly shy one. "I don't think anyone's ever seen him—not to my knowledge," Phillips said.

George's lack of visibility has not effected the staff's devotion to their paranormal presence. In keeping with one of many theater traditions, just before moving from one building to another, the people associated with the Civic carefully swept the dust from the stage of their former home and deposited it at the new venue. They did not want to take a chance on leaving George behind. The first time the toilet in the men's room flushed when no one was anywhere near the washroom, they were satisfied that they'd been successful in transporting their very special entity.

Chapter

5

THE ROAD
WELL
TRAVELED

Urban legends are twice (at least!) told tales, rumors that have circulated so efficiently that their content has been accepted as fact whether it began that way or not. The spread of these stories is not only a fascinating phenomena but, thankfully for lovers of ghostly lore, the tales frequently revolve around ghosts.

Throughout history, legends have always served important cultural purposes. Today, because the vast majority of people live in urban centers, the modifier "urban" in the phrase "urban legend" has more to do with the events being contemporary than it does with the story taking place in a city. As we shall see in the following Washington-based tales, many urban legends take place in rural settings such as country roads. Whether the manifestations appear in isolated rural locations or on busy city streets, their stories make for thought-provoking reading.

Woman in White

A classic phantom hitchhiker story began to make the rounds just after the 1980 eruption of Mount St. Helens. Sightings of the roadside apparition, a lady in white, have been reported by some highly credible people, including Elizabeth Simpson of the University of Washington. She related an encounter experienced by her husband's young niece, Judy, who had been driving down the Olympic peninsula just four months after the eruptions in May of 1980.

The young woman had stopped to fill her car's gas tank at a service station. The pump jockey was friendly and the two began chatting. As they were saying goodbye, the attendant warned the woman not to pick up hitchhikers along the way—especially a woman in white. "There's been a woman in a white dress hitch-hiking her way up and down the I-5," he cautioned. "She gets in the back seat and predicts that the volcano is going to erupt again between October 12 and 14. Then she disappears."

By the last week in September, the story of the doomsday manifestation had made its way into the mainstream media. Many people reported that they had stopped to pick up a traveler who met the specter's description. The entity's warnings were becoming more and more specific. The eruption, which was to occur in mid-October, would lay waste to a 100-mile radius.

Even the local police were alerted to the possibility that motorists might report encountering a vision. Eventually, the sightings became less and less frequent until they stopped completely. Once her deadline of the middle of October had passed and her prediction had not come to fruition, the mysterious woman in white was not seen again.

Ghost or Angel?

A supernatural being, much like the one described in the last story, began appearing the previous spring in the Mount Vernon area, considerably north of Mount St. Helens. A motorist reported picking up a female hitchhiker. She told him, "God is coming"— and then, before the man's eyes, she disappeared into a cloud of smoke. He was understandably shaken, and he reported the incident to the local police. After assessing the information, the officers concluded, "There were no facts, nothing to go on, so we dropped it."

Even though half a dozen other drivers in the area had similar encounters, it was suspected that the vision was simply a figment of the drivers' imaginations. Not all of the authorities shared this assumption. For example, Reverend Paul Jacobson, Minister of the Viewcrest Assembly of God in Mount Vernon, felt that the being was an angel—a messenger from God.

Given the number of years that have now passed, it is likely that we will never know exactly who or what the disappearing hitchhiker really was. Of course, the image may have been the result of overactive imaginations, or it may have been an angel, but it seems to me that a strong argument could be made for it having been a ghostly apparition. Ghosts have a long history of being highly visible one moment and gone the next—even if the spot where they had just been seen was inside a car, barreling non-stop down a highway.

Phantom Driver

In many regards, the following ghost story could be categorized as an interesting twist on that staple of urban legends, the phantom hitchhiker story. This one, however, is also remarkably different in a variety of ways. For one thing, the names of those involved in the ghostly encounter are known for certain, as are the time and place the events occurred. And, most importantly, in this story the driver of the vehicle is the phantom—the hitchhikers are real people!

What I believe we have here is a true ghost story, one that ends with many thoroughly bewildered people. To begin the tale, we must travel in our imaginations to Seattle—the Seattle that existed for two nine-year-old friends, Ernie Poindexter and Meredith Wright, on a September Saturday in 1963. Although summer was over and school had started—thereby managing to ruin their fun from Monday to Friday—the two little boys still had the weekends to spend doing as they pleased. On that particular Saturday morning, what they wanted most of all was to go to a movie that was playing in a downtown theater.

Life was not only simpler in those days, but safer; the lads thought nothing of standing at the curb with their thumbs out until a trucker stopped to give them a lift. Despite the "No Riders" sign that was clearly posted on the side of the truck's cab, the driver waved Ernie and Meredith over. "Jump in," he shouted over the noise of the engine. "I only have a couple more deliveries to make before I head downtown. I'll bet that's where you boys want to go, isn't it—to the Saturday afternoon movie?"

Nodding in enthusiastic agreement, the boys opened the truck's back door and climbed in. Moments later, the truck, with the giggling boys in its cargo hold, pulled out onto the road again. They'd only gone a few blocks when the driver once again steered his vehicle over to a curb. Meredith and Ernie heard the driver turn off the truck's ignition and pull on the hand brake. Seconds later, the man opened the back gate and pulled out one of the cartons surrounding the boys. As he did, he assured Ernie and Meredith that he'd be right back.

"Just this delivery and one other before we start toward downtown," the man told them. "By the way, my name's Phil, Phil Cullen." Being too young to realize that the man's introduction had been their cue to identify themselves, the boys merely smiled and nodded, indicating their silent agreement to wait patiently for Phil's return. As they waited, they heard what sounded like another truck pulling up directly behind them. To their horror, it became clear just seconds later that the second truck had slammed into the one they were sitting in. The impact sent Phil's truck, with the boys helplessly trapped inside, hurtling down a steep hill.

Packages and boys were roughly tossed around the back of the truck as the runaway vehicle sped along on what could only be a collision course with disaster. Terrified, the boys clung to each other.

Suddenly, the truck lurched to the left and slowed somewhat. "Don't be scared, boys," yelled a man's disembodied—and obviously stressed—voice. "Just hang on tight. I'm trying to jam the brakes on."

With eyes as big as saucers, the two youngsters stared at one another. What was happening? How could anyone have managed to get behind the wheel? Ernie, being the braver of the two, reached up and slid open the little window between the cab and the cargo hold. There was no one in the front of the truck, yet the steering wheel held straight and true as though guided by an invisible hand.

At Ernie's urging, Meredith scampered up beside his friend and peered through the window. The boys watched in amazement as the horn rim in the steering wheel depressed itself and the horn blasted a warning to pedestrians. As it barreled down the hill, the vehicle swerved, first this way and then that, in order to avoid obstacles and certain calamity. Over and over again, the horn honked to warn pedestrians in the area. Eventually, when it reached the bottom of the hill, the delivery truck came to a safe stop.

Moments later, a terrified and breathless Phil Cullen pulled open the back door to his vehicle. He could scarcely believe his eyes. There, sitting huddled together, were the two boys he had left in the back of the truck. Aside from being frightened, they were none the worse for wear. Soon, dozens of people were running to the truck, anxious to find out if there was any way they could help. All were certain that anyone inside the ill-fated truck would have been, at the very least, seriously injured.

"Good thinking, lads," Phil declared. "If you hadn't steered the truck like you did, you might not have survived that little ride."

When they finally found their voices, both Meredith and Ernie explained, as best they were able, that they hadn't steered the truck, that they'd been in the cargo bay where Phil had left them the whole time. For a moment the man merely stood, silent and still, staring blankly in apparent disbelief. Then a bystander spoke up. "The boys are telling the truth," he said. "I watched the entire episode. No one was in the truck's cab."

"How did the truck make it down the hill without hitting anything?" asked Phil.

"I don't know how to explain it, sir, but I can assure you that there was no one at the wheel—no one who could be seen anyway," the man added, shaking his head and walking away.

And so, on that September Saturday in 1963, the lives of Ernest Poindexter, Meredith Wright, and anyone in the path of the runaway truck were saved by a phantom.

Lifesaving Entity

Although Rufus Porter would later become a noted American journalist, in December of 1960 the man was utterly down and out. Tired, hungry and discouraged, he was making his way west from Spokane toward Seattle in the hopes of finding work. His method of transportation was the only one he could afford—Porter was riding the rails, stowing away on freight trains headed in the same direction as he.

On this particular night, the only rail car Porter could access was both empty and open. Because the train would be making its way through the Cascade Mountains that night—and because the temperature was predicted to fall below zero—Porter knew there was a very good chance that he would freeze to death and not live to see the morning. Even so, he could see no alternative. Staying behind at the side of the road offered even less protection from the elements.

Porter climbed aboard. If only there'd been some mailbags or other freight in the car, he could have built himself a protective nest. The fact that his senses were numbed by lack of nourishment and extreme fatigue was, in an odd way, a blessing. His conscious mind could not fully comprehend the horror of his life-threatening dilemma.

As the train jerked to a start and began to noisily pick up speed, Porter was thrown against the wooden side of the car. "Here goes nothing," he thought, and settled back to let fate do with him what it would. He stared aimlessly at the passing countryside, occasionally escaping into unconsciousness.

Porter was fully awake, however, when the train approached Leavenworth. He rubbed his eyes to make sure that they weren't playing tricks on him. There, at the side of the track bed, was a work camp. Porter's hopes soared. He had learned from experience that he could seek both shelter and food at such camps. Grabbing his gunnysack, he jumped from the moving car in the practiced way of the hobo. He let himself go limp and rolled into a deep bed of snow that had accumulated in the culvert between the tracks and the tents.

Stumbling in the deep snow, his movements hampered even further by his deteriorated physical state, Porter made his way the few yards back to the tents. He headed for the largest of the makeshift shelters, intending to call out for help when he got close enough. And the poor, destitute, half-frozen man may actually have done that. We'll never know exactly what Porter did as he approached the refuge, because his next conscious memory was of waking up in a comfortable cot, covered with wool blankets.

Struggling to open his eyes, Porter caught a glimpse of a man standing at the foot of the bed on which he was lying.

"Thank you," he mumbled, hoping he sounded even a fraction as grateful as he felt. The man merely nodded and Porter drifted back to sleep. Some time later he blinked his eyes open again. His caretaker was standing in the same place, still staring down at him.

"Who are you?" Porter inquired.

"I am your brother," the stranger responded.

Too groggy to stay awake, or to make any sense of the man's cryptic reply, Rufus Porter closed his eyes once again. It wasn't until he woke for a third time that Porter was able to stay awake. By then, the man who had been watching over him was in another area of the tent, seemingly working away at something in the corner. As consciousness imposed itself more and more, Rufus became aware that the man was cooking. Better still, he was cooking bacon and eggs. Perhaps he would share!

Shakily, Rufus pulled himself up to a sitting position. As soon as he did, the man was beside him, handing him a full plate heaped high with bacon, eggs, hash brown potatoes and thick slices of buttered toast. It had been weeks since Rufus had seen a proper meal, and he ate ravenously, without so much as a thank you to the man who had prepared and served the meal. Once the plate was empty, Porter looked up somewhat sheepishly.

"Thank you," he said with great sincerity, before repeating his question of some hours ago. "Who are you?"

"I am your brother," the man said.

Not knowing what else to do, Rufus Porter began to make himself ready to depart the work camp and the man who had undoubtedly saved his life. As he took his leave, Porter again thanked the kind stranger.

"I appreciate all you did for me," Rufus told the man. "I'm sure we've never even met before and yet you've probably saved my life. Thank you for your kindness. If I had any way of repaying you, I would."

In reply, the man merely repeated, "I am your brother."

Refreshed, Porter made his way directly to Leavenworth, where he met up with a few of his acquaintances, men with whom he had ridden the rails on previous occasions. He described, in detail, the work camp at the side of the tracks and the good Samaritan who had saved him from hypothermia and starvation.

"You're crazy, Porter," one of the oldest in the group declared. "That camp hasn't been there for years. The guy you're talking about sounds like Old Joe, but he's been dead for ages. You must've been further out of your mind than you thought you were to believe that you were staying in places that don't exist and talking to dead people."

Confused, Rufus Porter resisted the temptation to make any sort of a reply. He merely set out for what he thought would be the final leg of his trip westward to Seattle. Instead, he found himself strongly drawn back toward the east. He realized that he could not rest easily until he saw that work camp again. He needed to prove to himself that both the place and the person had, in fact, been real.

When he arrived back at the spot from which he had set out that morning, Rufus Porter could only stand stock still and stare. There, before his eyes, were the tumble-down, weathered ruins of a work camp that must have existed many seasons before. Nowhere was there any sign of recent habitation, nowhere was there any trace of life. Even so, the future journalist knew that this was the exact spot where, just hours before, he had received life-saving care and protection from what he now realized was a ghost.

Disappearing Date

Eugene Trundy will remember one particular day from 1986 for the rest of his life. It was the day he found himself passing through Stillwater, just east of Redmond, Washington. That afternoon, Trundy befriended a young woman named Jill Parker. The two spent some time together in the afternoon and, before they parted, Eugene asked if he could see her again that evening. Even at the time, Jill's answer struck Trundy as being a little odd. She replied, "I hope so."

Trying to overlook Jill's strange choice of words, Trundy asked where he might pick her up for their date. She named an intersection and suggested that they meet there, as she lived just along the street from that corner. After agreeing to rendezvous at the meeting spot at 7:30 that evening, the pair parted.

Trundy had some dinner, freshened up, and arrived at the designated corner a little early. He wasn't at all worried to see that Jill had not yet arrived. When she still hadn't shown up by 8:00, however, he became concerned. He went back to the diner where he'd eaten his meal and began to make inquiries about the woman he had been hoping to meet. Trundy was surprised to find the waiter, a man named Bill, pouring him a glass of beer, even though he had not asked for one.

"Drink," Bill told him. "And when the glass is empty, there's more where that came from. It's on the house."

Trundy had no way of knowing that Bill, and the others who worked at the diner, had heard many stories about Jill Parker over the past 10 years. It seems that Jill had committed suicide in 1976, immediately after hearing the news that her young son had been in a fatal car accident.

Ever since, people around the diner will occasionally hear stories from visitors to their community who claim to have been conversing with a woman meeting Jill Parker's description. A few times there were even reports of Jill and her son being spotted walking together toward their house—before simply vanishing.

After hearing what Bill had to say and realizing that he had made a date with a ghost, it's likely that Eugene Trundy was glad to have the unasked-for glass of beer.

A Haunted Intersection

Ellensburg, located at almost exactly the geographic center of the state of Washington, is as pretty a community as you're likely to find anywhere. And it always has been—except for the intersection of 7th Avenue and Pine Street. For years, that corner was widely acknowledged to have been haunted "with a dark aura."

This ghost story dates back to the days of the Wild West. One day in 1895, a group of vigilantes decided—without bothering to engage in the time-consuming protocol of a proper trial—that a particular father and son, the Messrs. Vincent, were guilty of murder. With considerably fewer thoughts of justice than of expediency, the mob hanged the two men at the corner of 7th and Pine.

For many years thereafter, and with great justification, the people in the community avoided that part of town after dark. Although phantom images of the wronged men were never seen, their horrible cries were said to have echoed throughout the neighborhood. Their ghosts called out for the help and lawfulness in death that were denied them in life. By now, those distraught energies seem to have dissipated and the area is no longer thought to be haunted.

Headlong into Forever

Collecting ghost stories has, in one way, been a bit like the experience of parenting. The more personal involvement I've had, the less sure I have been that I understood any of the theories inherent in the practice. For example, if a ghost is what's left behind after a human life has ended, then how do you account for sightings of ships that sank hundreds of years ago?

One comfortable explanation of that phenomenon might be that such apparitions are merely spectral images, mirages concocted from a combination of sea spray and overactive imaginations. But I wish to extend an invitation to ponder a similar, but even more puzzling, manifestation—that of phantom trains. Ghost trains have been seen by many reliable and experienced trainmen. The following is one such tale.

In 1890, Tom Cypher, an engineer with the Northern Pacific Railroad, was driving locomotive number 33 through a particularly dangerous stretch of track in the Cascade Mountains. We can never know exactly what happened as he piloted his train toward Eagle Gorge. We only know that the train derailed and plummeted to the gorge floor below, killing everyone on board.

From that day forward, all the train engineers who followed in Cypher's path redoubled their vigilance in that area, especially at night. They were all too aware that the stretch had already taken a colleague's life and that the least little mistake could result in the Gorge taking their lives as well. Even more troubling, though, was the terrifying image that many experienced trainmen saw as they approached that fateful spot on the single-track line—another train, heading straight toward theirs at top speed.

Just as the two trains seemed about to collide, the ghostly loco-motive would vanish into thin air. History tells us that this phantom train continued to run on the tracks between the Hanson Dam and the town of Lester until at least 1892, because it was then that the Seattle-area newspapers carried a full report of the phenomenon as told to them by engineer J.M. Pinckney. To Pinckney's utter terror, the phantom locomotive had charged right at his own train.

It was not until Pinckney noticed that the lights on the front of the locomotive that was bearing down on him were multicol-ored that he realized he was seeing a ghost. You see, in those days, train headlights were illuminated by kerosene, which casts only a dull brown glow.

It would seem that Tom Cypher, engineer of locomotive num-ber 33, was not only doomed to suffer a dreadful death but also to endure the torture of endlessly re-enacting his fatal accident and striking terror into the hearts of his fellow engineers.

Train to Nowhere

Roughly halfway between Seattle and Tacoma lies Kent, Washington—and a more recent tale of a phantom train.

On a winter's day nearly 40 years ago, two employees of a local flower shop, a man named Thompson and an older woman whose name has been lost to history, were driving through Kent and making some deliveries. Thompson was at the wheel, and as he approached the train tracks he could hear the sounds of a locomotive. The sounds were very loud, so he assumed the train was quite close. Thompson slowed the car in anticipation of stopping at the level crossing just ahead.

When he had brought the car to a halt, roughly 10 feet back of the train tracks, Thompson experienced the surprise of his life. He also found out why the engine noises he'd heard had been so loud. Much to his astonishment, there, just in front of his car, huffing and puffing for all it was worth, was an ancient steam engine. Thompson had not seen one of those behemoths for years, and then only in a museum. He was fascinated.

In silence, the man and woman watched as first the engine, then the tender, and finally a string of passenger cars rolled past their waiting automobile. As each section of the train passed, Thompson was more and more amazed. This magnificent iron horse had to be a very special train on its way to a very special event—not only was the train itself unusual, but it was easy to see that the people inside were all dressed in old-fashioned costumes. In his excitement, Thompson did something he hadn't done since he was a kid—he waved to the folks on board. Much to his disappointment, even though he could see that each one of the passengers was staring directly at him, none of them returned his greeting.

By the time the tracks in front of his car were once again clear, Thompson found that his initial excitement had been replaced by an inexplicable feeling of having been chilled to the bone. When the noise and the dust created by the strange train had receded, he turned and stared at his companion, assuming that she would look as confused as he felt. Much to his surprise, the older woman was merely nodding knowingly.

As clearly and calmly as she possibly could, Thompson's co-worker explained that they had just witnessed a legendary ghost train. Some said the powerful steam engine pulled cars full of criminals. Others merely acknowledged that the startling apparition was a phantom locomotive, for nothing like it had existed on this side of the veil for a very long time.

Sisters in Spirit

You can be sure that the majority of Spokane's citizens in the late 1800s and early 1900s were not prim and proper sissies. For one thing, folks with a preference for the easy life would never have ventured away from their comfortable parlors in the East. And if by some chance a person with a delicate nature had chosen to set out for the wild and woolly West, the rigors of the trip would most likely have eradicated the last vestiges of their fastidiousness long before they reached Spokane. As a result, most of the residents in the eastern Washington city's early days were pretty hardy characters. Unnerving them was not an easy task.

It is ironic, then, that the sight of two haggard-looking women, dancing a silent duet on a stage in an opera house just outside Spokane, drove a grizzled old caretaker screaming into the night. Once you've heard the whole story, I have no doubt that you will understand his reaction.

Bella Rawhide and Timber Kate were "working girls" in the most corporeal sense of the phrase. They did a sort of song and dance show in many of the bars and saloons that dotted the West in the 1880s, but it was not for the performing arts that they were best known or most appreciated.

The women made a decidedly odd pair. Timber Kate must have been an arresting sight. She was a redhead who dressed in bright, shiny clothes. She was also, in a word, huge. She stood over six feet tall and was as strong as an ox. Furthermore, Kate didn't have a shy bone in her body. Some would have gone so far as to call her brazen, although never to her face—Timber Kate was, after all, widely known for her knockout punches.

Bella Rawhide was a blue-eyed blonde of average height. Where Timber Kate was both shrewd and quick to anger, Bella had a pleasant disposition and was, right to the end of her life, a pushover for a sad story.

This odd pair usually billed themselves as sisters. In her last years, Bella maintained that Kate was really her mother, but poor Bella Rawhide rarely drew a sober breath during that period, so it's probably unwise to put much stock in that allegation. The absolute truth about their biological relationship may never be known, but it seems likely that the women merely hoped the "sibling" designation would draw more paying customers.

Although their differences were many, Bella and Kate were inseparable for a great number of years. Together, they worked their way through the dance halls from Nevada to Washington and back. They had their sister routine down to a science. Timber Kate would travel to the next town and post notices about their upcoming performances. Bella would stay behind for a few days so she could tend to their outlandish dance hall costumes and tidy up whatever loose ends might remain. Upon reuniting, the women would do their show, seduce their customers, and then begin the whole cycle over again.

The strange pair had worked in this pattern for many years and probably would have continued to do so for quite some time if they had not fallen in love with the same man. Tug Daniels was the object of their affections, and they could scarcely have made a worse choice. Daniels was a con man who had had no interest in either of the women—beyond relieving them of their rather substantial earnings, that is.

Daniels decided to beguile Bella Rawhide first. The unsuspecting woman fell for his questionable charms hook, line and sinker. When Timber Kate saw what was happening she was furious, and, for the first and last time in her life, landed one of her famous haymaker punches against the side of Bella's head. When she regained consciousness, Bella was terrified of Kate and deeply worried about what form the other woman's jealous rage might take next.

The badly bruised Bella fled—with Tug Daniels in tow. The pair had traveled all the way to Carson City, Nevada, before they felt it was safe to stop.

Tug apparently wasn't one to earn a living, so the ever-resourceful Bella opened a bawdy-house and plied her well-honed and most marketable skills instead. Tug stayed with her for a while, perhaps acting as a forerunner of today's househusband. Soon, however, the lure of adventure called to him and Tug took off for parts unknown—taking Bella's savings with him. Not knowing what else to do, Bella Rawhide continued to operate her popular house of ill-repute.

Timber Kate had not fared as well. She had drifted throughout the West trying, without success, various approaches to making a living with her "talents," until one night she found herself in Carson City and on the doorstep of Bella's bordello. Once reunited, the duo immediately set about rekindling their volatile relationship over copious quantities of moonshine. It's not known whether Kate and Bella ever really tried to iron out their grudges. What is known, however, is that over the next several months they rarely spoke a civil word to one another.

Just when the women's once-positive relationship had deteriorated about as badly as it could have, Tug Daniels arrived back on the scene and managed to make the situation even worse. Before long a physical fight broke out. That match must have been something to see, given that the years had not been kind to any of the combatants. When Timber Kate lunged at Tug, the haymaker punch for which she had once been famous succeeded only in forcing her off balance. She fell against the knife Tug Daniels had extended in her direction, fatally ripping open her abdomen. Daniels fled, leaving the enormous woman to the indignity of bleeding to death on a whorehouse floor.

Bella was never the same after the death of her former partner. She took to drinking heavily and indiscriminately. Just a few months later, the smaller of the two "sisters" also died in the house. Her death had been caused by ingestion of a lethal dose of cleaning fluid.

And that, should have been the end of the tale about these two unusual pioneer women. But Timber Kate and Bella Rawhide's stories don't end with their deaths. The caretaker who was cleaning the Spokane-area dance hall all those years later recognized the specters prancing across the stage in the darkened dance hall—they were the ghosts of Timber Kate and Bella Rawhide.

Others reported seeing the image of a bedraggled-looking woman, meeting the description of Bella, stumbling and crawling through roadside gutters, clutching at her mouth and throat, trying vainly to extinguish the excruciatingly painful burning that would have resulted from drinking a poisonous liquid.

As unsettling as that phantom image would have been, there was a tobacconist who would, no doubt, have far preferred Bella's ghost to the vision he witnessed. That unfortunate man was a shopkeeper, whose name has been lost to history, and he actually suffered physical harm when he was targeted by the wrath of Timber Kate's wraith.

Late one evening, the man was locking up his shop and preparing to head home when a person moving around the side of the building caught his attention. At first, because of the dusk and shadows, he might have thought it was a man dressed in women's clothing, but a moment later he must have realized that the peculiar-looking stranger was, in fact, a very large woman.

Wondering what on earth the woman was doing, he approached her. As he did, the figure mysteriously vanished—leaving only a poster flapping in the evening breeze on the outside wall of his store. Annoyed at having an advertisement defacing his store, the tobacconist took hold of the paper at a corner and began to rip it off. His tidying was cut short, however, by a powerful sucker-punch to the back of his head. He crumpled to the ground, unconscious. Hours later, the poor shopkeeper was found where he had dropped, lying beneath a poster informing the public that the musical "sister" act of Bella Rawhide and Timber Kate would soon be arriving in town.

Now that you know the background to the incident, it's certainly easy to see why that caretaker at the dance hall near Spokane fled screaming into the night.

Presence in the Park

The Roaring Twenties were a wild time in Washington—and everywhere else in North America! The Great War had finally ended, leaving in its wake not only a booming economy but an entire generation of citizens ready to appreciate the economic upsurge and enjoy life more fully than ever before. And no two people were better prepared to take advantage of the newly created atmosphere of freedom than Tom and Eliza. They were young, they were ambitious, and they were engaged to be married. They were certain that their prosperity and happiness were assured—but to help fate along just a bit, the couple moved to the big city from the small town in which they had been raised.

Seattle in the 1920s was an exciting place to be. During the day, Tom worked at an insurance agency. He was intelligent and, perhaps more importantly, he was industrious. Although he was hired only to do clerical work, he welcomed every opportunity to show that he could do more.

Before long, Tom's hard work was rewarded; he was made a junior partner in the firm. On the afternoon of his promotion, Tom could hardly wait to see his beloved Eliza and share the terrific news. She could finally quit her job as a typist and the two could marry and start the family they both wanted.

The clock above Tom's desk seemed to take at least twice as long as usual to get to 5:00 PM. At quitting time, he all but flew from the office. The firm's senior partners were used to their young "apprentice" staying behind until all his work was finished. They were not upset, though. Quite to the contrary, they were delighted because they knew that he was rushing off to plan the rest of his life—a life that would include extraordinary loyalty to their firm.

By the time he arrived outside the building where Eliza worked, Tom was out of breath. He was also early. She would not be free to leave work for another few minutes. He took the time to compose himself, catch his breath and enjoy the anticipation of the moment. That enjoyment became so all-encompassing that when Eliza did make her way to his side, he was completely lost in thought.

For her part, Eliza was so pleased to see her fiancé that she did not notice the faraway look in his eyes. She certainly didn't expect that her simple, enthusiastic greeting of "hello" would startle Tom, but it succeeded in doing exactly that. His jumpy response told Eliza that her normally relaxed lover was bursting with excitement. She could hardly wait to hear his news.

Arm in arm, the young couple strolled through the darkening Seattle streets, planning the most wonderful future possible.

"And children, Tom—we must have children," Eliza declared as they climbed the Queen Anne Hill.

"We'll have the finest children in the world," Tom confirmed without hesitation.

Neither direction nor distance had meant anything to the couple as they'd walked and talked, but now, as they found themselves approaching Kinnear Park, they made their way toward a bench. The chatter between the two continued, but as Tom was extolling the sterling qualities that their future children would possess, Eliza slowly became more and more distracted. She thought she could hear the sounds of a baby crying somewhere very close at hand.

"It's just my imagination," she thought. "It's because we're talking about babies—that's why I'm hearing those cries."

Finally, the piteous wails completely diverted Eliza's concentration and she interrupted Tom to ask if he heard them, too. The still-excited man stopped talking mid-sentence and turned his head at an angle.

"Yes, you're right. There is a baby crying nearby," he confirmed.

The pair immediately stood up and began to move toward the plaintive sounds. But no matter how far they walked, they always seemed to be the same distance away from the disturbing noise. The sun had now been set for quite some time, and the growing darkness led the couple to assume that they were merely having trouble seeing the child among the shadows. Their own joy set aside temporarily, Tom and Eliza concentrated on finding the source of the cries. They could certainly not leave while an infant lay abandoned in the park!

Their search had, thus far, been fruitless and frustrating. When Tom and Eliza happened upon a policeman strolling through the park, they were relieved at the prospect of having someone in authority to help them in their mission. The couple hurried toward the uniformed officer.

In their mounting concern for the unseen baby's well-being, the two spoke simultaneously and in far too much of a mad rush to be understood. Even so, the policeman was calm. He knew exactly what it was that had this young couple so upset. They were merely the latest in a long line of people to hear the phantom cries of a deceased child—cries that were so poignant and real that he knew it would take quite a lot of convincing to call off the search party that these two were probably already envisioning.

Fortunately, he had done this before. With as much patience as he could muster, the kindly Seattle policeman explained that, no matter how diligent the search, no one could ever locate that particular crying baby. "It's a ghost," he stated simply. "Those cries that you heard were from another dimension. That child is no longer in this time or place—only his cries are left with us."

Even though it was twilight, the officer could tell by the expressions on their faces that the young couple was shocked by his words. He also knew that this was not the last time he would have to make this same explanation to concerned citizens. People had been hearing the little soul's cries for years, and they probably would for many more years to come.

When they were convinced that the policeman knew what he was talking about, Tom and Eliza left the park and headed to a downtown restaurant for a late dinner. The excited chatter that had marked their trip to the park had been replaced by stony silence. Although they felt they had little choice but to accept the policeman's words as truth, neither of them could quite believe what they'd just heard—neither the pitiful wailing nor the officer's chilling explanation for it.

Months, even years later, long after they'd married and started their family, Tom and Eliza would often discuss that memorable evening in Kinnear Park, wondering about the tiny infant responsible for the mournful crying that they, and so many others, had heard.

The autumn of 1929 did not bring much that was positive to the world. It did, however, mark the end of something negative. After that time, the phantom cries of the ghostly infant at the top of Queen Anne Hill in Kinnear Park were no longer heard. The child had gone on to his or her eternal rest at last.

Thanks to one couple's compassion, neither the tiny tormented soul nor its plight were ever forgotten. As soon as their own children were old enough to hear the story, Tom and Eliza told, and retold, the tale of their experience to their two sons. When those two boys grew into men, married, and had children of their own, they shared the true ghost story with those kids.

Because of this family's intergenerational storytelling, the suffering child has been given the attention that he cried out for—even after death.

Chapter 6

SEA LORE

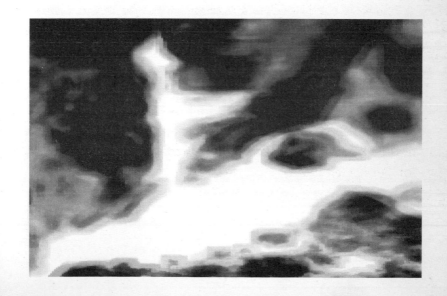

There are not as many instances of ocean-going tragedies on the Pacific as there are on the Atlantic. Even so, the West Coast is certainly not immune to shipwrecks, nor is it free of the ghosts that inevitably manifest as a consequence of maritime disasters.

Following are a few of the ghost stories connected to Washington's shores and the seas beyond.

The Haunted
Sea King

One of the most bizarre Washington sea tales began in San Francisco, just after the earthquake in the spring of 1906. No one has ever been able to come up with an accurate count of those killed by the quake and the fires it triggered. Many of the bodies simply disintegrated or became inextricably tangled up with the debris. During the rebuilding process, tons and tons of twisted materials were hauled to the shipyards and stockpiled. City planners hoped that ships dropping off cargo at the San Francisco Bay harbor could take on some of the detritus as ballast to balance their vessel before heading out for the next port on their journey.

The *Sea King* was just such a ship. She had delivered a heavy load of wood for use in San Francisco's reconstruction and, to keep the vessel balanced once the lumber was offloaded, took on an equal amount of the ballast that had been set aside for that purpose. After her stop in San Francisco, the *Sea King* steamed north to Seattle, where the ballast was unloaded in preparation for the next load of cargo.

As the dock workers shoveled out the ship's holds, they were horrified to discover bones mixed in among the rubble that had been used to weigh down the *Sea King*. Those who work on—or even near—the sea tend to be a superstitious lot, and finding human skeletons from the earthquake scattered throughout the ballast was more than enough to push most of these men over the edge. Even though there had been no unusual events during the voyage from San Francisco to Seattle, word soon spread that the ship was cursed. Soon, the sailors swore they could hear groans and other unexpected noises coming from the hold area of the vessel.

Despite being badly haunted from that point on, the *Sea King* had a long career up and down the West Coast, making many more voyages before being retired to the bone yard.

Phantom on Pier 70

One rather whimsical piece of local folklore has it that a handsome young captain and his clipper ship appear out of a highly localized shroud of fog or mist near Seattle's Pier 70. The twist in this ghost story is that the man and his vessel are only visible to those who are in the throes of despair. He speaks to everyone who sees the ship, encouraging the living to persevere and assuring them that their fortunes will improve. His visits are prophetic, because the luck of the dejected witnesses inevitably improves.

This entity and his ship are especially interesting because, judging from the detailed reports given, they appear solid and lifelike to the person who sees them—and yet remain invisible to everyone else.

Spirits Onboard

The *Equator* is now permanently docked at Everett, some 25 miles up the coast from Seattle. The beautiful old schooner serves as a museum, and, as might be expected of a ship that is more than 100 years old, it is haunted. The identities of two of the ghostly presences are, however, rather unexpected. Both Robert Louis Stevenson and King Kalakaua of Hawaii made themselves known to participants in a séance onboard the ship. In addition, ghost lights are frequently seen floating above the deck.

Photo Not Available

In 1949, Frank Nickerson of Seattle earned his living crewing for a local shipping company. Being an outgoing sort, he enjoyed a pleasant relationship with almost all of his co-workers. Rarely, however, did he actually become friends with the other men. A young man named Donald proved to be the exception to this rule. Frank was so taken by Donald that he invited the newcomer to enjoy a home-cooked meal.

As it turned out, Frank's wife (whose name, owing to the era in which this story was reported, has been recorded only as Mrs. Frank Nickerson) liked the youngster just as much as her husband did. As a result, Donald was a frequent dinner guest at the Nickersons' home.

Mrs. Nickerson prided herself on her ability as an amateur photographer, and during one of Donald's visits she suggested that she take his picture. Donald laughed and told her that no one could take a picture of him. The woman understood the youth to mean that no one could take a good picture of him and immediately accepted his words as a challenge to her skills with a camera.

"No," Donald declared in an attempt to clarify the misunderstanding. "No one can take my picture. There will be nothing on the film."

Nevertheless, Mrs. Nickerson set about trying to prove their young friend wrong. After taking two pictures each of her husband and of Donald, she put the camera away. Moments later, Donald left the Nickersons' house. Somewhat confused by what had just occurred in their home, the couple tidied up from the meal and set about spending the evening alone.

A few days later, Frank reported that Donald seemed to be avoiding him at work. He made this observation on the same day that Mrs. Nickerson picked up her film from the developer. She was extremely interested in seeing the results of her photography session during the evening of Donald's last visit. Although she had taken the young man's picture twice, both times occurring mere seconds after she had taken photos of her husband, there were no pictures of Donald to be found. She checked the strips of negatives and discovered that the two shots on the roll immediately following the portraits of Frank were completely blank. Donald, it would seem, had been correct. No one could take his picture.

What could account for this seeming impossibility? Could Donald have been a temporary visitor from a previous time, a man who was taken from this earthly plane too soon and had therefore returned as a ghost to enjoy what he had missed as a man? We can never know for certain, but this is not the only Washington-based tale of an apparently living creature that could not be photographed.

Many miles inland at the Turnbull National Wildlife Refuge, south of Spokane near Cheney, Jack and Katherine Healy and their two sons were enjoying an outing. The little boys found a snake, named it Slinky, and decided that it would make a wonderful pet. Unfortunately, their parents disagreed—all that would be allowed was a photograph of their father holding the snake. Katherine quickly snapped the pose, Jack put the snake down, and the family carried on with their activities.

Some days later they were reviewing the pictures they'd taken on the trip. They were, for the most part, pleased with the way the roll had turned out. One shot, however, that of Jack Healy holding the snake, had them all puzzled. Although the shot was perfectly composed and focused, close examination of the photo revealed that Jack's hands were completely empty.

Widow Still Waits

The sea has made more than its fair share of widows. For some of the bereaved, the grief was so devastating that they have gone on mourning even after their own death. This phenomenon is responsible for at least one haunted house in Seattle.

Early in 1966, Marlys Drews and her four sons moved into a house that was perched atop a hill with a view of Puget Sound that Marlys understandably described as "beautiful." The family settled in easily and were thoroughly enjoying their new accommodations until the very early morning of June 27, 1966. At 12:20 AM, Marlys was wakened from a deep sleep by the sound of someone calling her name. At first Marlys thought that she must have been dreaming, but when she was fully awake the woman realized that she could also hear someone walking up the stairs.

As most mothers would, Marlys assumed that one of her sons needed her and immediately got out of bed. Curiously, she found that the boys were all in their beds, fast asleep. The only thing that seemed amiss was the door to the area of the house that included the boys' bedrooms; it was standing wide open. Marlys knew for a fact that the door had been closed when she turned in for the night.

Despite the peculiarity of the situation, Marlys was not at all frightened. Quite to the contrary, she reported feeling "a strange sense of peacefulness." Slowly, she came to the realization that whoever had called her "was satisfied that I had heard the call." Feeling utterly secure, Marlys Drews returned to bed and slept soundly for the balance of the night.

The next morning, however, the events of the night were still on her mind. Once she had the children organized for the day, the young mother decided to phone a friend—a friend with psychic abilities. Marlys explained what had occurred in the night and waited in silence for a few moments.

"Is there an attic in your house?" the psychic inquired.

"No, not really," Marlys replied. "But there is a storage area under the eaves."

This was obviously the area that the psychic felt needed to be explored if they were to solve the mystery. The psychic immediately suggested that Marlys go up to that part of the house and look near the base of a rafter. "You'll find a picture there," she assured her friend.

Puzzled, Marlys did precisely as her sensitive friend had advised. Making her way up through the trap door, she hunted through the cramped, dark area as best she was able using a hand-held flashlight. After a few minutes in this unpleasant position, Marlys was about to return downstairs, thinking that her friend had been mistaken this time. Then, out of the corner of her eye, she saw something lying against the base of a rafter. She picked the object up and was amazed to find that it was a photo negative. Her friend had been almost completely correct when she had predicted that Marlys would find a picture. The snapshot negative could certainly be made into a picture quite easily.

As soon as she was back downstairs and in the daylight, Marlys held the negative up to a window. She could see a shot of a woman and two children. Judging from the clothing and hairstyles, the picture had been taken in the 1940s. The psychic was sure that it was the spirit of this woman that Marlys had heard.

Her curiosity piqued, Marlys began making inquiries around the neighborhood. One couple who had lived in the area for more than 30 years remembered an Italian couple who had raised two children in the house that was now Marlys's home. The couple's daughter had married and had children of her own. When World War II broke out, the young husband joined the merchant marine. To combat the inevitable loneliness she would feel in his absence, the wife took her children and moved back into her parents' home.

She and the children had just settled in when, on June 27, she watched a man carrying an envelope walk purposefully up the front walk. She instinctively knew what message the man was bearing even before she answered the door. Her husband's ship had been blasted by an enemy torpedo; there had been no survivors.

The young widow never fully recovered from her grief, the neighbors told Marlys. She lived with her parents for the rest of her life in the house that the Drews now called home.

Upon hearing the story of her newly acquired house, Marlys felt reassured. The sailor's widow had undoubtedly made the sounds that Marlys had heard that night. What's more, her ghostly visitor had manifested herself on June 27th—the anniversary of the sailor's death more than 20 years earlier.

Body Aboard

Hunters, Washington, located northwest of Spokane, seems like an unusual place to find the story of a ghost at sea—but that is exactly where this tale originated. Hal Browning, a resident of Hunters, was serving as a ship's plumber with the Military Sea Transportation Service in the 1950s. Throughout his career, Hal had made some good friends among the sailors and other tradesmen. One of those friends was Chief Electrician James Mason (no relation to the late actor). As Browning and the others aboard the *USS Marine Adder* set sail from Seattle on February 26, 1952, en route to Yokohama, they were saddened to hear the news that Mason had died early the previous week.

The first few days out on the *Adder* were busy ones for Browning. The rig had just recently been recommissioned and she required a great deal of work. As a result, all the tradesmen aboard were dog-tired by the end of their shift.

The fourth or fifth night out, Browning was so exhausted that he collapsed on his cot early in the evening and fell into a deep sleep. Some hours later, he was awakened by the sensation that someone had sat down on the edge of his bed. He opened his eyes and was shocked to see his deceased friend James Mason sitting beside him. Browning bolted upright in surprise. As he did, the ghost stood up, glided to the middle of the room, and "began to spin like a top—he whirled faster and faster and then vanished."

Badly shaken by what he had seen, Browning ran to find his roommate, Clarence Albeck, and tell him what had just transpired in their cabin. Albeck was not surprised to hear that their late friend's spirit had appeared—because Mason's remains, in the form of ashes, were stored with Albeck's kit. Albeck had not wanted to tell Browning for fear of upsetting his roommate, but he had volunteered to take the urn full of the dead man's ashes on this voyage in order to satisfy the electrician's final wishes— that he rest forever in the middle of the Pacific Ocean.

The next day, after saying a few fitting words, Hal Browning watched as Clarence Albeck tossed Mason's urn into the wake of the *USS Marine Adder*. His ghost was never seen again.

Haunted Marketplace

The ghosts haunting the ships' piers have proved to be considerably more tenacious. Every time the flesh-and-blood tenants in Seattle's Pike's Place Market think they have the place to themselves again, one of the ghosts makes a reappearance.

One shopkeeper, a man named Leon, discovered that he had seen one of the phantoms many times. He had always found the woman's demeanor to be odd—she made her way along the pier so slowly that she almost seemed to glide, and she was always looking straight ahead. It wasn't until the apparition came into view while Leon was chatting with some friends that he found out why the woman appeared to be, well, a bit different. "There's the ghost," his companion whispered. Even without this helpful hint, Leon would probably have figured out the enigma this time. As he explained later, "You could see right through her."

The ghost is generally believed to be that of a woman who sold woven baskets at the pier in the early 1900s. She has appeared in most of the stores in the market at one time or another, often startling the proprietors by either walking through a wall or seeming to evaporate right before their puzzled eyes.

Another materialization that many people have seen is commonly thought to be one of Chief Seattle's daughters. And no one seems to know the identity of the tall, handsome African-American man whose spirit haunts the market, while another ghost has been confidently identified as that of Arthur Goodwin, who was once the director of Pike's Place Market.

Perhaps the most charming entity, though, is the ghost of the dancer. He is a well-dressed man who is extremely light on his feet and who appears in a specific area on an upper floor of the market. It is believed that this spirit dates back to the Second World War and the dances that were organized at that time by Boeing workers.

Not all of the ghosts in the market are seen. Store clerks frequently report hearing phantom footsteps emanating from spaces that they know to be unoccupied. Seaside venues are not the only haunted stores in converted downtown spaces. Retailers and customers at the Freighthouse Square in Steilacoom have reported seeing the apparition of a man dressed in the clothes of a railroad worker, possibly a train conductor or a ticket agent. And at least one Freighthouse Square shopkeeper wondered if her store was haunted by a child-like spirit, because she would often find that small items she had used to decorate her store were rearranged in the night.

Chapter

7

SCHOOL
SPIRIT

If a ghost is psychic energy left behind after the corporeal body has left the earthly plane, then it's not much of a surprise to learn that school buildings are often haunted.

Teachers put an enormous amount of energy into their instruction, and most students, despite frequent protestations to the contrary, often invest an equal amount of positive emotion into their school experiences. Interestingly, Washington seems to have an inordinate number of haunted schools.

Haunted Halls of Learning

Many years ago, when classes for the new term at The Academy on Evergreen Boulevard in Vancouver began, the teacher welcomed what she thought was a room full of fresh new faces. After a period of instruction from the teacher and interaction among the children, the school bell rang. One of the boys who had been participating in the morning's activities immediately stood up from his desk and left the room. His departure was primarily noteworthy for the fact that he exited by walking through a solid wall. The little wraith was never seen again.

The haunted Academy is no longer a school, but on some occasions it is still full of students—or the ghosts of former students. Night workers at the facility, which now houses commercial enterprises, have reported hearing the sounds of children's voices coming from rooms that the workers know to be empty. Inevitably, when the workers unlock the room, the sounds stop as suddenly and mysteriously as they began. Worse, no amount of searching produces a rational, flesh-and-blood explanation for sounds they have all clearly heard.

Phantom footsteps are heard pacing on the top floor—an area that is now locked and consigned to storage. Some long-dead soul is apparently pacing back and forth into eternity.

The Monk's Manifestation

Although many would disagree, St. Martin's College, a private school in Lacey, is widely believed to be haunted by the ghost of a monk. The spirit was reportedly seen by a group of people standing in a fourth-floor hallway on an evening in the early 1990s. All those assembled watched in amazement as the monk's image strode toward them. Much to their surprise, he stopped and asked where he could find his students. Without waiting for a reply, the monk walked on, turned a corner and vanished. Until that moment, the presence had been so lifelike that everyone had assumed that he was a living human being.

The specter is thought to be the ghost of a young monk who plummeted to his death in the autumn of 1962. He may not be the only long-dead presence lingering at the school, however. A security guard who fell asleep one evening was startled awake by the sound of snoring—and it was not his own. Alarmingly, the guard could see that he was utterly alone in the room.

As befits a school setting, the ghost or ghosts at St. Martin's like to play pranks—usually by manipulating lights switches from an on position to an off position or vice versa. For the most part, though, the living and the deceased at St. Martin's coexist very peacefully.

Enigmatic Entity

Just after World War II, the Burnley School of Professional Art began conducting classes in a facility at the corner of Broadway and Pine in Seattle's Capitol Hill district. The building had served many purposes since its construction in 1907. A portion had even been used as a high school gymnasium, and it was this function that apparently caused the building to become haunted.

Legend has it that while a physical education class was being held in the gym, a fight broke out between students who had been playing basketball. Before the melee could be stopped, a student was dead. His spirit is generally accepted as the one haunting the building.

Budding artists and their instructors who used the facility came to call the presence Burnley. They became quite comfortable with the sounds of their resident phantom making his way up and down the hallways and creaky old stairs—except when they were alone in the building at night. Because they were visual artists, the students would have as many lights as possible turned on while they painted or sketched after nightfall. Despite the brightness of their surroundings, they could often hear a presence which they could not see. For this reason, many students passed up a second opportunity to work independently at the school in the evening.

Some sounds, such as a piteous moaning that a group of young artists heard but could not track down, were disturbing even when in the company of others and during broad daylight. The rustling noise made by a person flipping through a magazine did not frighten anyone—until the sound was investigated and found to have been coming from an empty room.

For a time during the late 1950s, an artist named Henry Bennett had his living quarters in the haunted building. When he was interviewed about his time with a wraith as a roommate, Bennett spoke very matter-of-factly. He acknowledged that when he went to investigate strange sounds such as someone walking or working in a particular room, he frequently found the area deserted. He also added that he had never felt afraid of the ghost.

In 1965, Suzy Smith (no relation to me), who was at that time collecting and writing true ghost stories, toured the haunted school with a group of highly regarded psychics. Their tour must have been an exciting one. The mediums were unanimous in their opinion that there had been a death in the vicinity of the building in the days when it had been used for sports. They also agreed that the ghost was from this earlier era. This information went a long way toward explaining the strange noises, such as the sound of the desks being dragged away, which were frequently reported in the area that had once been the gym. When people heard this racket, they inevitably investigated and always found the room and its contents as they should be—empty, with all the desks in place.

Later in the evening, Smith's group held a séance. Using a stool as the tool of communication, the corporeal beings present asked if there were any spirits in the room who wished to speak. In such situations, a spokesperson for the group typically asks the ghostly entities to tap the floor with the stool. The code suggested is most ften one tap of the stool legs for a positive answer, two for a negative response. In this case, however, the seemingly mundane little piece of furniture did not respond in the expected manner but jumped into frenzied action, banging and crashing around the room in a manner far too energetic to impart any discernable information.

As the furor was dying down, one of the psychics unexpectedly slipped into a trance. Judging from his monologue, the spirit of the murdered basketball player had entered his body. The poor soul was extremely distressed. He was not only angry that he was dead but also upset that time had continued to march forward since his death.

After that supernatural meeting, the spirits at the art school were, apparently, either much calmer or gone for good. Oddly, no story about a death in the building—much less the violent death of a young person—could be found in any of the records pertaining to building. In the final analysis, the haunting that took place at the Burnley School of Art was truly an enigma.

Permanent Roommate

Unfortunately, even living off campus is no guarantee of ghost-free accommodations at Washington schools. In the pretty community of Pullman, on the eastern edge of the state, an apartment that is usually occupied by students is also home to a ghost.

It's a large suite, most often shared by two or three people. When all of the roommates are home, there can be a fair number of footsteps sounding up and down the hall in the apartment. But occasionally occupants hear more sets of footfalls than there are tenants. One year this situation continued throughout the academic term.

The next year, the same three students moved back in. The ghost must have wanted to let them know that he was still in residence, too. As the three boarders sat in the living room on a completely still day, the front door to the apartment suddenly slammed shut with tremendous force. Even though they often left the door open, the incident never recurred. The sounds of phantom footsteps, however, continued to be heard, just as they had the year before.

The third year, one of the roommates found accommodations elsewhere, so a new person came to live at the haunted apartment. As it turned out, she and the suite were well matched. She had lived in haunted houses before and was well accustomed to ghostly goings-on. Perhaps this encouraged the spirit, because he began to ensure that the students were always aware of his presence. He would turn stereos on in the middle of the night and play with the cutlery in kitchen drawers.

This last incident left the tenants badly shaken. Although they found all of the kitchen drawers closed, they found the cutlery inside them to be in complete disarray—which was certainly not the way they had left it.

At this point, the roommate who was most familiar with ghosts tried to coax the presence to leave. Perhaps she was successful, as there have been no further reports of the haunting. It's equally possible, though, that the phantom is simply waiting for new friends to join him in Palouse Country's great beyond.

Lovely Lola

Central Washington University's Kamola Hall in Ellensburg has a long and mysterious ghostly tradition. The spirit's name is Lola, and it seems that a legend explaining her presence has sprung up around the rather obvious signs of a haunting.

The aroma of perfume will suddenly waft through a room full of men, none of whom have been out of the room for any considerable time. "It was like a woman walked past," one man explained. The windows in the room were closed at the time, yet all present were aware of the pleasant odor's sudden onset and its gradual fading.

The sweet-smelling lady has even been seen at least once. She appeared in a mirror, but when the young man who caught a glimpse of her reflection turned to see her physical image, he found that he was alone in the room.

A wonderfully poignant story has been created to explain the phantom presence in the residence. Lola, a student at Central Washington during the Second World War, is said to have taken her own life in Kamola Hall after being told that her lover had been killed in battle. Tragically, the young woman had been misinformed. Her fiancé was very much alive, but now, of course, Lola wasn't. Unfortunately, nothing in the way of documentation can be found to support this tale. What the legend lacks in accuracy is certainly make up in romanticism.

Lucky Haunting

Streeter Hall, at Eastern Washington University in Cheney, has been haunted since 1967—but after one failed attempt to identify the spirit, no one is any the wiser. As a result, the ghost is still referred to simply as "Lucky."

The apparition has been seen, heard and smelled. During 1989, a student adviser named Joe had a few very close encounters with Lucky. The first time, Joe was asleep in his room at Streeter when he heard noise from inside his wardrobe closet. If he was scared by that, we can only imagine the poor man's reaction to the events of the next two evenings.

As he lay in bed the next night, Joe heard the closet door close and latch—even though he could plainly see that it was already closed. On the third night, he listened in terror as the hangers in his closet banged and clanged if as though someone was swatting at them.

The haunting in that particular room ended abruptly. The next room to be haunted was occupied by an exchange student from Japan. Just as he had been in Joe's room, Lucky was loud and hungry for attention in the visiting student's quarters. This time the noises were accompanied by foul odors. And that particular student actually saw the figure of the ghost.

The specter has also been seen in the hallways and, at last report, was still active and noisy. The mystery of his presence remained unsolved.

Famous Phantom

Gonzaga University's ghost is probably one of the most famous in the state. The wraith has been the subject of many discussions, newspaper reports and even chapters in books. This well-recognized, see-through citizen of Spokane resides in the university's music room at Monaghan Hall—but the existence of the ghost pre-dates the school's use of the building. Although the haunted hall has been part of the campus since 1939, it was originally a house of classical Victorian design, which is somehow a fitting style for a classically ghostly presence.

The mid-1970s were extremely active times for this haunting, with the most intense paranormal activity beginning in the fall of 1974. A member of the cleaning staff who had just finished her duties in Monaghan Hall re-entered the building in the belief that she had left something behind. The place had been empty when she had left just moments before, but as soon as she opened the door, she distinctly heard a simple tune being played on the organ.

Puzzled, the woman made her way to the room where the organ was kept. The door was locked and, from what she could see under the door, the lights in the room were off. She unlocked the door and found the room empty and the windows locked. No one could have been playing the organ, but she was absolutely sure that this was what she had heard. The cleaning woman ran from the house in fear.

Not long after that incident, an instructor stood and stared in amazement as the locked handle on an interior door turned—and the door eased open at the will of an invisible hand. No one was on the other side of the door.

With any luck, that ghostly encounter prepared the instructor for what he was to witness the following January. That time he listened as flute music emanated from an empty first floor studio. Some weeks later, that same instructor was sitting at a piano in the haunted building. He found himself absently playing a melody on the keyboard. The cleaning woman who had heard the ghostly organ music the previous fall happened to be in Monaghan Hall as the instructor absently pecked out the tune. She hurried into the room thinking she'd catch a glimpse of the ghost. When she saw it was the instructor sitting at the instrument, she felt she had to explain her sudden arrival at the room.

A musical ghost haunts Monaghan Hall at Spokane's Gonzaga University.

"That's exactly the tune I heard being played on the organ," she exclaimed. It was only then that the instructor realized that he had, without consciously realizing it, been playing the ditty he had first heard played on the phantom flute.

On February 24, 1975, the musical spirit was seen for the first time. On that date, a group of five people assembled in preparation for an attempt to solve the tuneful enigma. While gathering outside the building, they saw a figure at a second-floor window. Because they had been assured that Monaghan Hall was vacant, they immediately rushed in to investigate. During a thorough search of the building, they found nothing—but according to some reports, all present were uncomfortably aware of an unseen presence.

A few days later, some of those people who had been involved with the search asked the ghost to leave. The ceremony was apparently interrupted by a concerned passerby who reported smelling something burning. They investigated and found nothing on fire, but the second-floor area smelled strongly of sulfur and ozone.

The ritual to rid Monaghan Hall of its musical spirits may have been successful. The only other supernatural incident in the building occurred nearly five years later. Guards on a routine patrol watched as a blackboard on wheels rolled toward them. As it pressed itself up against one of the men, the other guard pushed it away. Of course, one could blame the freakish event on the combination of gravity and a very old house. Or one could blame something a bit more eerie. If a ghost was to blame, however, that prank seems to have been his last hurrah.

Night Shift

The ghost that is thought to be a resident of the old Spokane Technical Institute building has been a real pest. Because all of the encounters with the spirit have taken place in the late afternoon or early evening, it is thought that the ghost dates back to a time when the building was used as a retirement home. Before that the building was used as an elementary school, but neither the timing nor the activities of the ghost imply any association with children.

The Institute's administrative staff has reported hearing phantom footsteps making their way along the hallway and down the stairs. This phenomenon occurs long after everyone else has left the building for the day. In addition, a custodian named Ryan has occasionally encountered some very difficult working conditions. He had heard the phantom footsteps often enough to become almost blasé about them, but he was admittedly startled when these noises were followed by the sound of the school's front door opening and closing. When Ryan checked the door just minutes later, he found it securely locked.

On other evenings, Ryan was unnerved by the sounds of voices in the empty building. He has also stood outside the building and watched lights randomly turn on and off. Still, the presence has only truly interfered with his work once—by taking a full bag of trash and dumping it at the bottom of the stairwell.

During the day, the old place has always been as good as ghost-free, and now that the facility houses Apollo College, the phantom may have faded away permanently.

When this building housed Spokane Technical Institute, it was inhabited by a pesky phantom.

Lightly Haunted

Many reliable witnesses have reported seeing a ghost in Everett High School's auditorium. In 1969, during a production of the musical *Carousel*, a student identified only as Mark T. climbed a ladder to the highest point in the stage area. He needed to secure a rope that had mysteriously come undone. Without the leverage guaranteed by a taut rope, the stage crew would not have been able to close the curtain at the end of the act. In a matter-of-fact manner, Mark made his way up the ladder. The second he reached the top, however, he abruptly shifted his hands and feet from the rungs to the smooth outside of the ladder, sending him sliding to the floor below in a matter of seconds. Those watching Mark's strange behavior remarked that he was as "white as a ghost." It was fully five minutes before they were able to calm him into some semblance of coherence.

The teacher-supervisor on duty, Mr. Reber, scoffed at the boy's claim that he had seen something supernatural. His mocking skepticism lasted just a few minutes, though, because when he looked up to the spot where the youngster had been, he saw a strange orb of light shining in an area where was no power.

Another time, almost the reverse situation occurred. A teacher who was completely alone in the building tried to remain calm when a spotlight turned on—and followed his every move while he walked around the auditorium. When students made fun of the man's sighting, he dared one or more of them to spend a night alone in the place. A young couple accepted the challenge, but left before daybreak after watching the spring-loaded seat bottoms of rows and rows of chairs fold down as though invisible patrons were sitting down to watch a nonexistent performance.

Teacher Bill Williamson was responsible for processing the

photographs for the school's yearbook. To complete the task on time, Williamson stayed in the school one night until nearly midnight. More than pictures developed that evening. While Williamson worked in the empty building, he distinctly heard a classroom door opening. Reasoning that the night janitor had come back to retrieve some forgotten article, the teacher paid no attention to the sounds—until he heard noises that seemed to indicate that there were many people in the building. Convinced that someone was playing a trick on him, the teacher went to investigate. He saw absolutely nothing—but felt a sudden draft of icy cold air move over him, even though there were no doors or windows open.

Williamson searched the entire building, but found that he was still completely alone. And yet the noises continued! Grabbing a portable light, Williamson retraced his steps. He planned to catch the jokester by flashing the light in his or her eyes.

Suddenly a door at the end of the room flew open with enough force to dent the wall behind it. Williamson aimed the light; the beam illuminated the shadow of a man—but nothing solid that could have cast such a silhouette. With that, Bill Williamson had seen more than enough. He fled from the school vowing to accomplish all of his future tasks in daylight.

The only clue to the identity of the ghost is the legend of a construction worker who supposedly fell to his death during renovations to the auditorium area.

Chapter 8

PHANTOMS WITH A MISSION

As I noted in the introduction to this book, some ghosts are apparently present so they can accomplish specific missions.

The following stories are Washington-based examples of such project-oriented specters.

Grocer Makes Good

This ghost story is probably the most heart-warming one I've ever heard. Picture, if you will, a little neighborhood five miles northwest of Spokane during the winter of 1931-32. The Great Depression had cut a swath through many people's lives, most certainly through the lives of Jacob and Mattie Belle Denton.

Try as he might, Jacob could not find a way to support his wife in their hometown. Just days before Thanksgiving, feeling he had no alternative, the man struck out to look for the proverbial greener pastures. Knowing how difficult it was for him to leave, Mattie could not bring herself to tell Jacob that she had just discovered she was pregnant. That knowledge would only have increased his burden. As it was, he was leaving her with no money. He took what little cash they had to help him on his journey.

Jacob had, however, arranged for a small line of credit which Mattie could draw on at the local grocery store. The proprietor was a kindly man who had always been good to his customers, including the Dentons, during these terrible times. He assured Jacob that the young man need not worry about Mattie's well-being while he was gone. The grocer would see to it that the woman had provisions for as long as she needed them, even if that meant exceeding the credit limit that had been established.

Agreeing that Jacob would send for Mattie as soon as he found work, the pair parted tearfully. At first, the young wife kept herself as busy as she possibly could. She took walks around the neighborhood and cleaned the little two-room house until it shone. As the pregnancy advanced, she had less and less energy. In a matter of weeks, it was all she could do to drag herself to the corner grocery store every few days. She soon became too weak to make the trip, but by that time, getting there would not have done her much good anyway. The line of credit that Jacob had established was already at its maximum. Mattie's pride would not allow her to ask for any additional generosity.

Without food, of course, Mattie's energy stores and strength waned even more quickly. To make matters worse, the fuel needed to power the heating stove had run out. The woman was not only destitute but cold and so weak from illness and hunger that she could barely get out of bed by herself. She had no friends or family nearby to call upon, and she had not heard from her beloved Jacob since he said goodbye. Like the terrible economic times around her, Mattie Belle Denton fell into the depths of depression.

She spent a solitary, miserable Christmas huddled in bed with the covers clutched over her. On December 31, as the clock struck midnight and 1931 became 1932, Mattie was sure she would not live to see the end of the week, much less the end of the New Year.

On New Year's Day, as she lay in bed under as many covers as she could find, Mattie was certain that she heard a knock at the door. Because she was not expecting any visitors, Mattie thought, "It's come to this, then, has it? I'm so sick that I'm hallucinating. Perhaps death is close at hand, and perhaps I am better off for it."

Using every ounce of strength left in her being, Mattie slowly shuffled to the door of her icy house. She called out, asking who was there, but found that her voice was so weak that it could not possibly have been heard on the other side of the door. Shuddering with the frigid blast of air that blew past her when she pried the door open, Mattie stared out onto the front step. There was no one there. Confused and even colder than she had been before, Mattie was about to close the door when she noticed three cartons on her doorstep. Beside them were a pair of five-gallon cans.

"Glory be, Jacob's found a way to get supplies to me," the grateful woman exclaimed. With more determination than strength, Mattie brought the supplies in. Once she had completed the task, she collapsed on the floor in sheer exhaustion. As soon as she was strong enough, Mattie began opening the boxes, giggling like a schoolgirl. Here was everything she would need to get her through the weeks ahead—meat, potatoes, bread, butter, eggs, canned goods. And the five-gallon containers that she had barely been able to lift were filled to the brim with heating fuel. Nearly giddy with relief, Mattie set about making herself the first meal she had seen in nearly a week.

After a few days of nourishment, Mattie found she was able to get up and move around. Every day she silently thanked Jacob for having been so resourceful in getting the food and fuel to her before it was too late. As the first month of the New Year wore on, however, there was no word from her husband. She began to worry again. Where was he? Surely he would get word to her soon. What would she do if she ran out of food again? Perhaps Jacob would not ever be able to get back—or even to get additional supplies to her. She began to ration her remaining food carefully and to berate herself for having been so greedy when the cartons had first arrived.

Despite her determined attempt to stretch what little food and fuel was left, the day eventually came when Mattie Belle Denton's larder was once again bare. Terrified, the woman took to her bed. As she sobbed silently into the pillow, she thought she heard a knock at the door. Straining to listen for the knock to come again, Mattie wiped her eyes and made her way to the door. As she had done all those weeks before, she called out to ask who was there. Again, there was no answer. Peering tentatively through a crack in the door, Mattie decided she must have imagined the knock, for there was no one there. As she prepared to close the door against the chill air, she again saw what she had seen a month earlier— three cardboard cartons and two metal containers. Here was another month's supply of groceries! She began to believe she would survive after all.

No sooner had she eaten than Mattie fell into a fitful sleep, only to awaken several hours later in terrible pain. Thinking that her stomach was having difficulty digesting the large meal, Mattie tried to make her way to the bathroom. It was then that she discovered the reason for her pains. She had miscarried the baby and was no longer pregnant. For several days after the tragedy, she lay in bed, near death herself. Eventually, she felt strong enough to get up and get herself something to eat, and she began to feel confident that she would at least live through this awful ordeal.

Some weeks later, Mattie was strong enough to finally venture out of the house. Because she had been cloistered and inactive for so long, even a little bit of exertion was exhausting. The first day she was only able to walk to the end of the block. The second, she made it a little further along. So it went until eventually she was able to make her way to the neighborhood grocery store. She wanted to go in and say thank you to the owner for having made good on what she presumed was Jacob's request to deliver the food and fuel.

When she came to the shop, Mattie pushed against the grocer's heavy glass door. Much to her surprise, she found that it would not open. Thinking that she must still be weak from her illness, the woman gave the door an extra push. The resistance was total. The door was locked. Mattie stood back in bewilderment. The grocery store that she'd frequented when she was well—that had kept her alive when she was ill—must have recently gone out of business. The shop windows were papered over. It was evident that the place was vacant.

As she stood trying to make sense of what she was seeing, a passerby stopped and asked Mattie if she was all right.

"Yes, I'm fine," she replied. "But did the grocer move?"

"Don't you know?" the stranger asked. "We're having to go all the way to the A&P store in Spokane for groceries now. The grocer died just before the New Year. His old place has been locked up for all of 1932."

Mattie nodded mutely and slowly began to walk home. She needed time to process what had happened over the last two months and what she had just learned. If the grocer had died, then who had brought those life-saving supplies to her door? After wracking her brain for a sensible answer, the woman smiled at the thought that kept popping back into her mind. Perhaps the old grocer's ghost had brought her some supplies from beyond. If nothing else, the silly thought kept her amused while she went through the motions of her empty life.

Weeks later, still as puzzled as ever by what had happened, Mattie answered another knock at the door. This time the arrival that was waiting for her on the doorstep was even more welcome than the supplies. There stood Jacob, home at last.

Mattie's joy at seeing her husband lasted only a moment. The man looked terrible. He was dreadfully thin, his clothes were nearly threadbare, and he had holes in his shoes. Jacob had ridden the rails all the way to California and back but had not found work. The situation was the same wherever he stopped. Work, and even food, were in tragically short supply. He'd had virtually no way to feed himself. He certainly hadn't been able to make arrangements to get food to Mattie. Why, he had only stayed alive on the journey home by nibbling on seeds he found along the way. He still had a handful of the seeds remaining in his pocket.

Jacob's relief at being reunited with his wife was so profound that he vowed they would never separate again. After sharing their first meal together in months, the couple made their way out into the yard surrounding their house. It was spring now and the soil outside was rich. They planted the few seeds that Jacob had not eaten on his way back from California.

As the weeks wore on, their garden flourished. They were able to trade and barter some of their bumper vegetable crop with a family living in a nearby tent who were raising chickens.

The Dentons not only made it through the Depression but also made lifelong friends with other survivors. Of course, none of them could afford to pay for any sort of entertainment, so they would instead gather in one of their homes and pass the time by telling stories. No matter how many times they heard it, the Dentons's friends never grew tired of hearing how the grocer's ghost had made good on his promise to Jacob by delivering food and fuel to the Denton's front door for weeks after his own death.

Fire Phantom

For a time in the late 1800s, the entire community of Goldendale, in the extreme south of Washington, was haunted by an angry spirit. In 1887, Henry Timmerman had been convicted of a murder that had been committed the year before. Feelings ran so high in this case that authorities kept having to reschedule the man's hanging, worried that the execution would create an angry and dangerous mob.

Finally, on April 6, 1888, Timmerman was hanged in Goldendale. Everyone thought Timmerman was guilty—everyone, that is, except the condemned man himself. Until the moment the hangman's noose was slipped around his neck, Timmerman vigorously protested his innocence. Seconds before the rope snapped, severing the man's spinal column and ending his life, Henry Timmerman vowed to return. He would come back, after death, to the town that had wronged him and extract his revenge.

Not many months later, all the buildings in the town's downtown core—including the jail where Timmerman had been held and the courthouse where he'd been tried and convicted—burned to the ground. Most of the residents of the badly damaged town were sure that the ghost of Henry Timmerman was responsible for the fire.

Revenge of the Wraith

They called him Oldie Neil—ironic, really, when you consider that the poor fellow didn't even live to see his 19th birthday.

Oldie might not have spent many years walking this earth as a mortal, but he certainly stayed around long enough as a ghost to make a number of people rue the day that they ever laid eyes on him.

Despite his youth, Oldie was married and the father of two. He was also a homesteader who had a spread south of Spokane, near Rockford, tight up against the Utah panhandle. His future looked promising: Oldie had planted a good field of wheat, and he had chickens and pigs, too. Those who knew him admired him for both his drive and his honesty. Oldie had been the victim of a few crimes but had never committed one himself.

Unfortunately, seven angry vigilantes (the Gentry twins, Wes Smithley, Bert Northrup, Fritz Tharp, Abe Murfin and Nate Collier) did not have all of these facts when they rode up to Oldie's house on a warm spring evening in 1882. All they had was a bunch of misinformation that they had taken away from the drunken ramblings of the town's ne'er-do-well, Sam Tate. Earlier in the day, Tate, who had been three sheets to the wind as usual, had implied that Oldie Neil was responsible for the recent outbreak of horse thieving and cattle rustling that the town had suffered.

Mob mentality always requires a scapegoat, and Tate's inebriated nonsense provided a name. But if any of those self-appointed lawmen had bothered with even minimal formality—such as pausing long enough to question Oldie Neil for a few moments— they would no doubt have discovered his innocence.

Unfortunately, fairness and justice are never high priorities for a posse. Not long after they'd first ridden onto his property, the seven fatally misguided men succeeded in hanging Oldie Neil from a convenient tree. Their evil deed done, the vigilantes rode back to town. To a man, they all needed some good strong shots of whiskey. They'd hanged other men, but never before had they been cursed as they committed their crime. None of them could shake the echo of Oldie Neil's dying words from their minds.

"You'll wish you had shared this hanging tree with me," Oldie had snarled, just seconds before the rope around his neck tightened. "You'll all die screaming."

Back in town, the murderers immediately made their way to the saloon. For a while, they drank in silence, intent on calming their nerves and washing away their guilt.

Abe Murfin was the first of the guilty to find his voice. "My God, what have we done?" was all he could mutter. Abe was also the first of the fatally misguided, self-appointed lawmen to die. Abe had been dead for several days by the time his wife found his decomposing, half-eaten corpse in a trough of pig slop on the Widow Neil's property. His killer was never found.

Wes Smithley had been the next man to speak on that spring night in the saloon. He turned to Samuel Tate and declared, "You made us hang an innocent man."

Wes, who had worked all his adult life in a sawmill, was crushed to death a few days later when a skid of logs broke away. The owner of the mill was mystified. All of his equipment was in excellent shape, and if any of his employees knew their way around a load of logs, it was Wes. No one ever determined what had caused the fatal accident.

Wes Smithley was barely in the ground when another of the vigilantes met his maker. Nate Collier was behind his six-horse team, plowing one of his fields. His wife, Mary, was beside him at the time. She later reported that the horses suddenly reared up, toppling the disc of the plow on top of Nate. The trunk of his body was sliced through. The former vigilante bled to death within minutes.

For years afterward, Mary Collier puzzled over the incident. She told anyone who would listen, "I can't imagine what spooked those horses so. It was like they had seen a ghost."

By now the survivors responsible for Oldie Neil's murder were on guard. They realized that the young man's spirit would not rest until it had taken revenge on them all. For this reason, Bert Northrup worked cautiously around his farm. He waited for a day when not even the slightest breeze blew before he climbed up the 60-foot tower to oil his windmill. He had no sooner reached the top when a single strong gust of wind came whipping out of nowhere, sending Bert's body plummeting toward the hard, unyielding ground below. The undertaker reported that every bone in Bert's body had been broken in the fall, and he added that the way the neck had been snapped was "just like he'd been hanged."

The three remaining members of the group that had stolen Oldie Neil's life were, by now, running scared. One of those three, Fritz Tharp, had read a piece in the local newspaper about Bert Northrup's fatal "accident." That night, Fritz fell into a fitful slumber. In the middle of the night, he woke up in a cold sweat, having dreamed about his own death. Badly shaken, he jumped from his bed and stumbled across the room toward his jug of whiskey. In the darkened cabin, the frightened man stumbled over his kerosene heater. The shack, which old Fritz had called home for many years, was instantly engulfed in flames. When his charred remains were found, it was said that the bones of his fingers were gripped across his throat as though he had been choked.

By now, almost all of the men who'd had a hand in Oldie Neil's unjust demise were dead. Only the Gentry twins, Tim and Fred, remained alive. Terrified by the thought of waiting for Neil's ghost to take him, Tim Gentry put a gun to his own head. But even his end was not swift, because he was so nervous that his hand shook and he botched his own suicide. It took him several long, agonizing hours to die. A witness was later quoted as saying, "He died a dog's death."

Fred Gentry was nearly crazy with anguish. He was the last of the cursed men left alive. He turned himself over to the local sheriff, explaining in nearly incomprehensible language that he had been cursed and was being pursued by a ghost. Understandably, the sheriff committed the raving man to a lunatic asylum, where he died after weeks of screaming that he was being licked by the fires of hell.

In 1903, a reporter from a Washington newspaper heard the blood-curdling ghost story and decided to investigate it for himself. His first order of business was to ride out to the tree where Oldie Neil had been hanged. When he couldn't spot the tree, he questioned some locals and discovered that the tree had been blasted into splinters when it was struck by lightning. Even worse, the townsfolk told the reporter, the lightning strike had also taken a man's life. Sam Tate, unconscious from drink, had been lying at the base of the tree when the lightning bolt hit.

The ghost of Oldie Neil had extracted his revenge and made good his dying curse.

Wild Ghost Chase

Ghost stories are, by their very nature, baffling. Some contain particularly enigmatic elements that make those stories more mysterious than others. The following tale certainly falls within the "more mysterious" category—it concerns the manifestation of a person who is about to die rather than one who is already deceased. As if that weren't enough to set this ghost story apart, it is also a geographically diverse narrative that begins in Winnipeg, Manitoba, Canada.

The year was 1937, and a young shoemaker named Emmanuel White was about to wed his beloved, Alice. Emmanuel was very much looking forward to being married. Not only did he love Alice with all his heart, but, because his own father had been killed along with many other men in an industrial accident when Emmanuel was just a child, he longed to create a secure home of his own. He was even hoping to become a father one day.

The Whites had not been married very long when, in the middle of the night, the husband woke up screaming. Initially incoherent from the terror he felt, Emmanuel concentrated on returning his breathing to a normal rate so that he could tell his concerned wife about the terrible nightmare he'd just suffered.

Trying to appear calmer than he felt, Emmanuel began by telling Alice that the dream had been about his father.

"But your father's dead, my love," Alice said, trying her best to soothe her badly shaken husband.

"But Alice, we don't know that for sure," he cautioned. "There were so many bodies found on that day that no one was able to accurately identify the remains in the rubble. I've always wondered if my father might not have lived through that dreadful accident and used it as an excuse to leave my mother and me. Now this dream seems to be confirming my suspicions."

Several hours later, Emmanuel's mind finally settled sufficiently to allow him to go back to sleep. The next morning, however, he was still terribly troubled by the vision he had experienced. At breakfast he described his nightmare to Alice.

"My father was at a lumber mill," Emmanuel explained. "He was dying and calling for me. I know it was just a dream, Alice, but it seemed so real."

"It might have seemed real, but it was only a dream," Alice counseled. "You'll have to try to set it aside and concentrate on the life you're living, not on these terrible visions of your father."

Emmanuel knew his wife was right and tried to put the awful images out of his mind. And, to a large degree he was successful— until a few days later, when he had the vivid nightmare for a second time. He woke up in a cold sweat and was again unable to get back to sleep.

Over the next few years, Emmanuel White suffered with that recurring dream many, many times. Each time the vision of his dying father filled his sleep, the images became more and more real. Then it happened. He was working, grinding the heel of a shoe, when the dreadful scenes that had been haunting his slumber played out before his waking mind. Unable to bear the tension any longer, he turned off all of his equipment, locked the door to his shop, and headed for home.

Alice was surprised to see her husband home in the middle of the day, and she was even more surprised by his evidently agitated state of mind.

"Get some things packed," he barked. "We have somewhere to go."

Frightened by her husband's unfamiliar abruptness, Alice silently obeyed. Less than an hour later, they were in the car and heading west out of Winnipeg. It was not until they were clear of the city that Alice sensed Emmanuel was finally relaxed enough for her to ask where they were headed.

"West, I have to go west," he told her. "My father's working at a logging camp somewhere on the West Coast. That much I'm sure of."

Three days later, the young couple arrived in Seattle. Emmanuel pulled in beside a telephone booth and immediately began scanning the yellow pages. He searched the listings for lumber outlets and began working his way down the page, phoning each company. With every call he introduced himself and asked if a man named Douglas White worked there. The young man's supply of dimes was running dangerously low when a lumber company receptionist finally assured him that, yes, a Douglas White worked for her company.

Emmanuel jumped back into the car. "I've found him, Alice," Emmanuel exclaimed excitedly. "I've found my father!" He steered back out onto the road. Forty-five minutes later, the couple reached the address he had copied from the phone book. Unable to contain his excitement any longer, Emmanuel switched off the ignition, threw the driver's side door open, stepped out of the car, and turned to look at a sight that took his breath away. There, before his eyes, stood the building from his recurring nightmare. He would have known it anywhere.

In his state of shock, Emmanuel didn't take notice of any details apart from the building itself. He didn't notice the ambulance parked at the curb or the workers scurrying around. To Alice, the activity clearly indicated that an accident had just taken place at the mill. With sudden clarity, Alice finally understood the reason Emmanuel had felt compelled to come all this way.

Those dreams had been messages from Douglas White, the father who had so long ago deserted his familial responsibilities. His soul had somehow sensed that the end was near and had called out for the son he had missed so much. Emmanuel White, inspired by a nightmare, had driven thousands of miles, only to arrive at his father's side just as the older man lay dying on a stretcher. The accident that killed Douglas White had been a freak one. A saw blade cutting its way through some timber had inexplicably shattered, flinging deadly shards of razor sharp metal at Emmanuel's father with great force. This had happened just moments after Emmanuel's phone call. No one except Douglas White had been injured even slightly.

Douglas White's doomed spirit had somehow reached out to his only living relative to create a truly bizarre ghost story.

Dead Ringer

Sometimes the messages we received from "beyond the veil" are so subtle that we are only faintly aware of their transmission. We don't see an image, hear a disembodied voice, or really notice anything much out of the ordinary. Anything, that is, except an inexplicable urge to visit a particular place or, perhaps, a strong feeling urging us not to leave home on a certain day. We may rush to label as "intuition" what is actually a communication from the spirit world.

In the spring of 1964, Peggy and Harold Carey were embarking on an adventure. Harold, an engineer, had just accepted a commission in San Francisco. The position required that he live in the city, so he and Peggy set out to drive to the Bay Area from their home in Delaware.

Not surprisingly, they had carefully planned their route long before the date of departure. Harold was surprised, therefore, when some miles into the journey, Peggy asked if they could visit Seattle. The city was considerably further north than they had planned on going—but they had plenty of time, so Harold readily agreed.

"The drive down the coast will be gorgeous," Peggy assured her husband. "And I'm afraid that if we don't see Seattle on this trip, we never will. Somehow not seeing that city just seems like a terrible shame to me."

Without further discussion on the topic, the couple plotted their course anew and continued along. They arrived in Seattle on a Saturday and were delighted with their first impressions of the city. Peggy was especially full of enthusiasm and kept suggesting that they take one turn or another, just to see where the road ahead would lead them.

When they drove slowly past a small neighborhood shopping center, Peggy suddenly became very agitated.

"Stop the car, Harold," she pleaded.

Surprised, the man steered the car to the curb and watched in confusion as his wife jumped out of the car. Scurrying around to the driver's side, she tugged the door open.

"See that church across the street? The sign out front is advertising a flea market for this afternoon. Let's go poke around for some bargains," Peggy suggested.

Although his wife's behavior was peculiar, her enthusiasm was contagious. Harold joined her immediately. The basement room in the church was lined with tables covered with all manner of items, large and small. As though directed by an irresistible force, Peggy moved directly to one particular stand, where she lost no time in picking out a plain gold ring from a basket of trinkets.

"How much for this?" she asked the woman standing behind the table.

"I'd like to get five dollars for it, but if you're not willing to give that much, you can have it for whatever you think it's worth," the vendor replied.

Silently, Peggy handed over a five-dollar bill. Turning to her husband, she said simply, "Okay, Harold, we can go now."

Later that afternoon, the couple checked into a motel just south of Seattle. After enjoying a leisurely dinner, they returned to their room to get ready for an early bedtime. They wanted to be refreshed for an early start on the next leg of their trip the next morning.

Just to have something to do, Peggy took her new jewelry purchase out of her purse and began to polish it. Suddenly she cried, "My God in heaven! I don't believe it—I don't believe it!"

"What's the matter?" her husband asked with a mixture of concern and irritation in his voice. Peggy's outburst had startled him.

"Read the inscription inside this ring, Harold," Peggy demanded. "I've just bought my own mother's wedding ring—the one that was stolen before she died. She had been promising it to me ever since I was a little girl. The ring was even in her will, but by the time she passed away, it had been gone for nearly 10 years."

Even though circumstances dictated that she had to do it silently and unseen from beyond the grave, Peggy's mother made sure that she kept her promise to her beloved daughter.

Grisly Looking Ghost

If you should ever happen to be out walking in Steilacoom on a dark and stormy night, you may cross paths with the ghost of a certain Mr. Bates. The wandering apparition of J.M. Bates has haunted several areas of Steilacoom for more than a century and a half. The spectral presence is harmless, unless one counts the inevitable fright that Bates's ghost gives people when they first see him. There's no denying that he is a grisly enough sight to give anyone a start, what with the hangman's rope and noose that strangled him still dangling from his neck. But you really need not fear Bates, because the poor deceased man means no harm.

When he was alive, J.M. Bates was a pauper and a simple man. He certainly didn't have a lot, but he didn't need much. After all, he lived in one of the most naturally beautiful spots in the country during uncomplicated times. Bates's only possession was a cow, and he treasured this animal above all else.

One day, Bates discovered that his beloved cow was missing. Sick at heart and raging with anger, Bates ran to the main street, which in those days was lined with saloons. Knowing that most of the men in the town would recognize his distinctive cow, Bates began asking if anyone had seen the beast. It wasn't long before someone volunteered that he had noticed a wealthy man named Andrew Byrd walking beside an animal that bore a strong resemblance to Bates's missing cow.

Bates caught up with the accused on the street and confronted him with the allegation. Byrd expressed no guilt and claimed to have no knowledge whatsoever of the theft. His denials only succeeded in inflaming Bates's anger further. In a rage, J.M. Bates drew his gun and shot Andrew Byrd. As Byrd lay dying, he pleaded with those who had gathered around not to punish Bates for the crime. It was Bates's simplicity and anger that had made a murderer of him, the fatally injured man protested, but J.M. was not a bad man.

The crowd was not nearly as magnanimous as the victim had been. Just moments after Andrew Byrd passed over to the great beyond, J.M. Bates was arrested and thrown into the Starling Street cells. Some hours later, a mob of vigilantes broke into the jail and captured its sole inmate. They bound the man's hands and feet, put a gag in his mouth, threw him on to the back of a horse, and rode directly to the woods with their prisoner. When they came to a suitable tree, they hanged the defenseless man.

The very next day, Bates's cow was seen grazing at the side of the railroad tracks. Shortly after that first sighting, word began to spread through the town that the man who had originally persuaded Bates to believe that Byrd was a thief had fled. The townspeople were finally able to piece together the whole story. Two wronged men were dead and the only truly guilty party had escaped to freedom.

Byrd's soul must have passed peacefully into the afterlife, because no one has ever seen his spirit. Bates's ghost, however, with the bloodied noose still dangling from his broken neck, has been seen wandering the streets. Most of those who have witnessed the apparition say he seems to be on an eternal search for his much-adored cow.

Cousin Bids Adieu

A man whom we shall simply call Don lives in the pretty south-central community of Richland. Don has lived a full and varied life—a life that has even included one extraordinarily profound ghost-sighting. The incident occurred early in the morning of November 15, 1971.

"I clearly saw the face of my cousin … near the foot of my bed," Don explained. "He said, 'Don, I have died.' Then his face disappeared. As far as I knew at the time, my cousin was alive and well."

Understandably troubled by what he had experienced, Don said nothing about his vision. "Four and a half hours after my psychic experience, the mail arrived. In the mail was a letter from my cousin's widow." Don did not have to open the envelope to know what message it contained. His cousin had died one week earlier.

Meets with Approval

Stan Towers, of Yakima, was a devoted son. In the early 1960s, his father, who was then quite elderly, was dying. Stan looked after the old man with great affection until his father's condition became too severe to be treated at home. Even after his father had been moved to a comfortable nursing facility and began receiving competent, round-the-clock care, Stan visited as often as he possibly could.

The young man's devotion was even more admirable considering that he was, during those same months, also dating Nancy, the woman who would eventually become his wife. As is the case with many courting couples, the pair left much unsaid. Stan spoke of his father so fondly and so frequently that Nancy longed to meet him. Because she did not wish to intrude, however, she kept her eagerness to herself. Ironically, Stan very much wanted to introduce Nancy to his father but didn't wish to impose on her. Sadly, Mr. Towers died before the two young people were completely comfortable communicating with one another. As a result, the two most important people in Stan Towers's life never met—at least not when they were both alive.

Several days after the funeral, the deceased man and his future daughter-in-law first laid eyes on one another. Stan had taken Nancy to see the house he had just inherited. As the couple sat chatting together in the living room, they were startled to realize that they had both heard a third voice.

"Its humorous tone was distinct," Nancy recalled. "But the words were not. I glanced toward the hall … and there he was, Stan's father."

The apparition stared at Nancy for a few seconds before smiling at her and then "melting away." Both Stan and Nancy realized that his father had come back to make their unspoken wishes come true. Nancy and her father-in-law had met, despite the usually effective twin obstacles of shyness and death.

(Stan and Nancy are pseudonyms. Their real names are in my files. All other details of the events are reported exactly as they occurred.)

A Ghost With a Purpose

On a Friday the 13th in the early spring of 1940, Earl, Don and Harold Willits set out together for the mountains of the Cascade Range to climb a peak known as Three Fingers. The young men had grown up in the area, not far from Mount Pilchuck, and were experienced climbers. Their planned trek on this occasion would total nearly 30 miles of hiking and climbing, so they decided to head out in the evening, camp overnight, and complete both the climb and the descent at a leisurely pace on Saturday.

It was 7:30 in the evening when they parked their car near Boulder Creek. Each wearing a backpack and carrying an ax, the trio set out on the first part of their hike. By 10 PM, they had found an ideal spot at which to spend the night—an abandoned lean-to, complete with a set of four bunk beds. Earl Willits took one of the top bunks and found that there were so many cracks in the roof of the old structure that, with his head resting on the pillow, he had a clear view of the night sky. He remembers watching "patches of white fog rise in eerie swirls from the ponds that lay in the valley." Earl fell asleep enjoying the unusual perspective.

It was several hours later, Earl estimated, that he awoke with a spine-jolting start. "Every nerve in my body tingled," he recalled—although, at the time, he had no idea why he should be in such a state. Seconds later, he opened his eyes and stared right at the reason for his sudden flood of feeling. There, floating directly above him as he lay on the top bunk, was the disembodied face of a man.

Understandably shaken, Earl had only a moment to size up the features that were peering intently at his own. He estimated that the features were those of a man of about 20. The face had several days' growth of beard, but the most striking feature was its pair of deep blue eyes. They were made even more striking by the fact that the apparition's face was also blue. Judging from its pinched nostrils and white mouth, the blue hue had been caused by extreme cold.

"Can I help you?" Earl asked the image. With that, the ghostly face vanished.

Earl did not get back to sleep that night. He was too puzzled by what he'd seen and too absorbed with pondering the possible significance of the sighting. Earl was afraid that someone was in mortal danger and was trying, perhaps in the only way he could, to get the attention of the men in the lean-to.

At breakfast Earl told his brothers about his experience. They were both sure that he had dreamed the whole episode, but Earl knew better.

The brothers broke camp and proceeded on their way to the summit. After hiking a distance of roughly seven miles, they met up with a ranger. The man advised them to change their route—the one they had planned to climb was far too dangerous at this time of year. He offered to guide the Willits through an alternative route. The brothers happily accepted the man's offer.

The ranger, chatting amiably while they climbed, explained why he had been posted in the area. Apparently another group had tried to climb the very trail that the brothers had been headed toward. One member of that party had lost his footing and slid to his death at the bottom of a crevice.

Earl whirled around to face the ranger. "What did that person look like?" he demanded.

The ranger explained that the climber had likely died on impact—and that by the time the rescue party had reached the poor man, "he didn't look pretty." Despite the man's caution, Earl insisted on a description. "He was about 20 years old, and he had about a week's growth of beard and the bluest eyes I've ever seen."

The three brothers stopped in their tracks. Without speaking, they all came to the conclusion that they now had an explanation for Earl's strange vision of the night before. Surely the young man's spirit had come back to warn the brothers not to travel on, that it was too dangerous and that they, too, might lose their lives.

The three men thanked the ranger for his kindness and told him that they had decided to head back to their base camp for now. Perhaps they would try the climb to Three Fingers on another occasion. Not many hours later, an enormous avalanche crashed down from the peak they had been heading toward. Had the Willits brothers not interpreted and heeded the ghost's warning, they would have met certain death.

Further Reading

Christensen, Jo-Anne. 1995. *Ghost Stories of Saskatchewan*. Toronto: Hounslow Press.

Davis, Jefferson. 1999. *Ghosts and Other Strange Critters of Washington and Oregon*. Vancouver, WA: Norsemen Ventures.

MacDonald, Margaret Read. 1995. *Ghost Stories from the Pacific Northwest*. Little Rock: August House Publishers.

Salmonson, Jessica Amanda. 1992. *The Mysterious Doom and Other Ghostly Tales of the Pacific Northwest*. Seattle: Sasquatch Books.

Salmonson, Jessica Amanda. 1995. *Phantom Waters: Northwest Legends of Rivers, Lakes, and Shores*. Seattle: Sasquatch Books.

Smith, Barbara. 1999. *Ghost Stories and Mysterious Creatures of British Columbia*. Edmonton: Lone Pine Publishing.

Smith, Barbara. 1993. *Ghost Stories of Alberta*. Toronto: Hounslow Press.

Smith, Barbara. 1998. *Ghost Stories of Manitoba*. Edmonton: Lone Pine Publishing.

Smith, Barbara. 1999. *Ghost Stories of the Rocky Mountains*. Edmonton: Lone Pine Publishing.

Smith, Barbara. 1996. *More Ghost Stories of Alberta*. Edmonton: Lone Pine Publishing.

Smith, Barbara. 1998. *Ontario Ghost Stories*. Edmonton: Lone Pine Publishing.

North America's colorful history is full of spine-tingling ghost tales that will have you checking under the bed, behind closet doors and in the basement. Haunting tales involve many well-known government buildings and landmarks, many of which are still being used. Stories range from the return of long-dead relatives, to phantom footsteps in unused attics, to whispers of disembodied voices from behind the walls.

Collect the whole series!

Ghost Stories of the Rocky Mountains
by Barbara Smith

Banff Springs Hotel • Denver's Unsinkable Molly Brown • the Frank Slide • Warren Air Force Base and more.
$10.95 U.S. • 1-55105-165-6 • 5.5" x 8.5" • 240 pages

Ghost Stories and Mysterious Creatures of British Columbia
by Barbara Smith

Ogopogo • Sasquatch • Vancouver's Vogue Theatre • the Dunsmuirs at Victoria's Craigdarroch Castle and more.
$10.95 U.S. • 1-55105-172-9 • 5.5" x 8.5" • 240 pages

More Ghost Stories of Alberta
by Barbara Smith

Cronquist House • Deane House • Hillhurst School • Fort Saskatchewan Jail and more.
$11.95 U.S. • 1-55105-083-8 • 5.5" x 8.5" • 232 pages

Ghost Stories of Manitoba
by Barbara Smith

Winnipeg's Walker Theatre • the Virgin Mary at Cross Lake • Hotel Fort Garry • St. John's Anglican Cathedral and more.
$11.95 U.S. • 1-55105-180-X • 5.5" x 8.5" • 240 pages

Ontario Ghost Stories
by Barbara Smith

Dundurn Castle • London's Grand Theatre • Baldoon • Canada's Hockey Hall of Fame • Algonquin Park and more.
$11.95 U.S. • 1-55105-203-2 • 5.5" x 8.5" • 240 pages